PRAISE FOR
YOU ARE ANOINTED

You Are Anointed is a powerful tool for believers who want to
be established in God's destiny for their lives.

CHÉ AHN
SENIOR PASTOR, HARVEST ROCK CHURCH
PASADENA, CALIFORNIA

You Are Anointed provides great understanding about how to walk, grow
and be more effective on our spiritual journey here on Earth.

SHARON ANN BARNES
NATIONAL DIRECTOR OF MINISTRY
WOMEN OF FAITH, INC.

You Are Anointed is destined to be a widely sought-after textbook
on the subject of anointing. Barbara Wentroble has given the
Body of Christ an astounding work. I highly recommend it.

KINGSLEY FLETCHER
SENIOR PASTOR, LIFE COMMUNITY CHURCH
RESEARCH TRIANGLE PARK, NORTH CAROLINA

Barbara Wentroble's book is not only timely, it is also a great
resource for the Church. In her down-to-earth, practical style,
Barbara shares truths and insights in a way that is easy to grasp.
You Are Anointed will equip you and encourage you to reach for
the anointing God has for *your* life!

JANE HANSEN
PRESIDENT, AGLOW INTERNATIONAL
EDMONDS, WASHINGTON

This book is must reading for anyone who desires to serve
God more effectively. An intensely practical book packed with faith-
building testimonies, *You Are Anointed* reveals how every believer
can walk in God's power. May He use this book to raise up a new
generation of anointed ministers, doing the works of Jesus
in their churches, businesses and neighborhoods!

ROBERT HEIDLER
SENIOR PASTOR, GLORY OF ZION OUTREACH CENTER
DENTON, TEXAS

Many believers talk about the anointing, but few understand
what it is and how it functions. *You Are Anointed* is a practical guide
that every Christian should read.

CINDY JACOBS
COFOUNDER, GENERALS OF INTERCESSION
COLORADO SPRINGS, COLORADO

Barbara Wentroble clears away the mystery and misunderstanding
that so often surrounds the concept of anointing. This primer
shows how to live with the power of Jesus' life permeating
every corner of your being.

DUTCH SHEETS
PASTOR, SPRINGS HARVEST FELLOWSHIP
COLORADO SPRINGS, COLORADO

You Are anointed

Barbara Wentroble

Renew
FROM REGAL

A Division of Gospel Light
Ventura, California, U.S.A.

Published by Renew Books
A Division of Gospel Light
Ventura, California, U.S.A.
Printed in the U.S.A.

Renew Books is a ministry of Gospel Light, an evangelical Christian publisher dedicated to serving the local church. We believe God's vision for Gospel Light is to provide church leaders with biblical, user-friendly materials that will help them evangelize, disciple and minister to children, youth and families.

It is our prayer that this Renew book will help you discover biblical truth for your own life and help you meet the needs of others. May God richly bless you.

For a free catalog of resources from Renew Books/Gospel Light, please call your Christian supplier or contact us at 1-800-4-GOSPEL or www.regalbooks.com.

Cover and Interior Design by Robert Williams
Edited by Kathi Macias and David Webb

LIBRARY OF CONGRESS CATALOGING-IN-PUBLICATION DATA
Wentroble, Barbara, 1943–
　　　You are anointed / Barbara Wentroble.
　　　　　p.　cm.
　　　Includes bibliographical references.
　　　ISBN 0-8307-2758-2
　　　1. Anointing of the Holy Spirit.　I. Title.

　BT123 .W45　2001
　234'.13—dc21　　　　　　　　　　　　　　　　　　　　　　　2001019621

1　2　3　4　5　6　7　8　9　10　11　12　13　14　15　/　09　08　07　06　05　04　03　02　01

Rights for publishing this book in other languages are contracted by Gospel Literature International (GLINT). GLINT also provides technical help for the adaptation, translation and publishing of Bible study resources and books in scores of languages worldwide. For further information, write to GLINT, P.O. Box 4060, Ontario, CA 91761-1003, U.S.A. You may also send e-mail to Glintint@aol.com, or visit the GLINT website at www.glint.org.

To my children, Brian, Lori and Mark.

The joy and delight you have brought into my life is immeasurable.

Your love and support are a constant source of encouragement.

My life is rich and full, as I see you fulfilling God's purpose for your lives.

Thank you for being you!

Contents

Chapter 1 8
The Smearing, Rubbing Anointing

Chapter 2 19
Do I Have an Anointing?

Chapter 3 31
Different Strokes for Different Folks

Chapter 4 43
All Can Prophesy—Including You!

Chapter 5 57
Apostolic Anointing

Chapter 6 71
Anointing for Intercession

Chapter 7 83
Corporate Anointing

Chapter 8 96
Marketplace Anointing

Chapter 9 109
Revival Anointing

Chapter 10 123
True and False Anointings

Chapter 11 135
Fat-Bull Anointing

Chapter 12 149
Faith for the Anointing

Chapter 13 161
Transferable Anointing

Endnotes 173

Chapter One

The Smearing, Rubbing Anointing

"Don't ever stand up and speak without the anointing."

What did the speaker mean by that? I had been invited by a friend to this meeting, and I had really enjoyed the songs, the people and the guest speaker's message—at least until she made that statement. I was puzzled. *What is the anointing?* I wondered. I had never heard that word used in my church.

Looking back now, I don't know why her statement bothered me. I had absolutely no plans of ever standing before anyone and speaking anything! I was one of the most shy, bashful, intimidated, introverted individuals on the planet. Still, for some reason, I had to know what this anointing was all about.

After the meeting, I drove to the home of a couple I had met a few months earlier. "I have to know about the anointing," I blurted out when they opened the door. My friends escorted me to their kitchen table and then pulled out an exceptionally large book. I had never before seen *Strong's Concordance*. We began looking up words such as "anoint" and "anointing" and continued until we had found every related word. After reading all the biblical references, my friends asked, "So what do you think the Bible says about the anointing?"

"It sounds to me as if the anointing abides within," I replied.

Satisfied for the moment with this new information, I drove home. I knew I could trust these friends, as I considered them seasoned servants of the Lord. After all, they had come into a new walk in the fullness of the Spirit three months earlier, whereas I had had a similar experience only two weeks before. Surely they were experts in the things of the Spirit!

My journey into understanding and operating in the anointing began that day—and it has not stopped. As a result, my life will never be the same.

A Picture of the Anointing

The word "anoint" comes from a Hebrew word meaning "to rub with oil . . . by implication, to consecrate; also to paint; smear."[1]

My husband, Dale, and I lived in Arizona for a couple of years when we were first married. During that time, I discovered that wood furniture could be damaged by exposure to dry air. Oil needs to be applied frequently so wood does not crack and become useless. I remember taking furniture oil and smearing it on the tables and bedroom furniture. I would then rub it into the wood. The oil penetrated the wood and helped it retain its original luster and value.

In biblical days, dried animal skins also needed to be smeared and rubbed with oil. Sometimes the skins were used as containers for liquids. If the skins became dry and brittle, they broke. Dipping them in water and then rubbing them with oil kept them soft and pliable, preserving their value and usefulness. Benny Hinn explains further:

Warriors had special ways to care for their weapons. For example, their battle shields, made of leather, had to be rubbed with oil to preserve them. The "rubbing with oil" is symbolic of the anointing, for when our lives are rubbed with the anointing of the Holy Spirit, they become useful for the kingdom of God.[2]

The Holy Spirit does a similar thing with believers. When we receive Jesus as our Savior, the Spirit of the Lord comes to live within us. Jesus then smears us with the oil of His presence. As we continue to walk in obedience to the Lord, the Holy Spirit rubs in a greater deposit of the life and image of Jesus. We are then able to reflect more and more of the character and nature of Jesus in our lives.

We must allow the life of Jesus into every part of our being.

Jesus is the Messiah, the Christ, the Anointed One. He wants to paint us with the anointing so we will look like Him. In fact, He wants to make us so slippery and greasy in the anointing that we will slip into His full purpose for our lives.

Chuck Pierce understands this concept. At the National School of Prophets on January 28, 1999, in Colorado Springs, Chuck prophesied:

The anointing. The word means to smear with oil, and if you will allow the anointing to rise within you, if you'll allow the smearing of the Holy Ghost upon you,

you'll make it through every narrow place that has been set before us.

God wants to bring us through every narrow place and establish us in our destiny. Our lives are neither accidents nor mistakes. We were in the heart of God long before we were in the thoughts of our parents. Before God put stars in the sky, before He caused the sun and moon to shine, before galaxies were set on their courses, God had us in His heart. He planned for our lives, and He has a destiny for each of us to fulfill. It does not matter what other people, circumstances or life experiences have told us. God has a special purpose for our lives, and He has provided the necessary spiritual equipment for us to be successful. This equipment is called the anointing.

Jesus employed the same equipment when He was on the earth. When He stood in the synagogue in Nazareth, He read from the book of Isaiah. He declared that the anointing was upon Him to help Him fulfill the Father's will:

> The Spirit of the Lord GOD is upon me, because the LORD has anointed me to bring good news to the afflicted; He has sent me to bind up the brokenhearted, to proclaim liberty to captives, and freedom to prisoners; to proclaim the favorable year of the LORD, and the day of vengeance of our God; to comfort all who mourn, to grant those who mourn in Zion, giving them a garland instead of ashes, the oil of gladness instead of mourning, the mantle of praise instead of a spirit of fainting. So they will be called oaks of righteousness, the planting of the LORD, that He may be glorified. Then they will rebuild the ancient ruins, they will raise up the former devastations, and they will repair the ruined cities, the desolations of many generations (Isa. 61:1-4).

This same anointing to bring good news is available to us today. I try to listen to the news on TV or read the newspaper for current world events, but rarely do I find good news. The media report murders, natural disasters, diseases, crime and all sorts of evil. All over the world people seem to be experiencing a sense of hopelessness. Jesus anoints His people—us—to declare the gospel, the good news, to those who live in a world of hopelessness and misery.

Jesus is the Healer. His anointing is necessary for us to be able to minister to broken people. Christ will give power to His people to heal broken hearts, and that anointing will break the power of depression, discouragement and mental torment.

My friend Barbara Yoder was preaching in South Africa when she received a request to pray for a lady named Joanne, who was in a mental institution in California. Barbara asked the congregation to pray with her, and pray they did! For 45 minutes, the people prayed fervently for Joanne's mind to be healed. At the end of that time of prayer, there was a sense among the congregation that the lady would indeed be healed. The very next morning Joanne stood at the door of the mental institution, healed and in her right mind. She was released and allowed to go home with her husband, because the anointing in the believers in South Africa had released the power of God in California.

Tormented captives are set free by the anointing. This same anointing not only frees individuals but also cities and territories. As we release the anointing and many individuals are restored, ruined cities are transformed by the power of God.

Throughout the Bible we see stories about changed lives, territories and nations. Transformation always occurred when God was present. His presence released people from bondage into freedom. That same presence is available today through the anointing.

God's desire is to transform the lives of all people. For this to happen, we, His people, His representatives, must allow Him

to smear and rub the life of Jesus into every part of our being—
He must live in our midst.

OLD TESTAMENT ANOINTING

God has always wanted to live in the midst of His people. In the
beginning, God came down and walked with Adam in the midst
of the Garden of Eden.

When Moses was called to the top of Mount Sinai, God gave
him instructions for building the Tabernacle: "Let them
construct a sanctuary for Me, that I may dwell among them"
(Exod. 25:8). In this verse the Hebrew word for "among" is *tavek*.
Some of the meanings of the word are "in the midst of, within,
the center, between, in the middle, out of."[3] The Israelites were
God's children. He loved them and wanted to dwell in their
midst. It was not His desire merely to be a God in heaven, sitting
on His throne, separated from His children. He wanted to live in
the very center of His family.

Moses directed the children of Israel to build the Tabernacle,
and the sanctuary was built according to God's specifications.
The builders used the right materials, the colors were correct,
and the dimensions were perfect. Even so, when the Tabernacle
was completed, nothing supernatural happened immediately.
The presence and power of God were manifest only after every
article in the Tabernacle and the priests had been anointed:

> And Moses examined all the work and behold, they had
> done it; just as the LORD had commanded, this they
> had done (Exod. 39:43).

> Then you shall take the anointing oil and anoint the
> tabernacle and all that is in it, and shall consecrate it

and all its furnishings; and it shall be holy. . . . You shall put the holy garments on Aaron and anoint him and consecrate him, that he may minister as a priest to Me (Exod. 40:9,13).

After everything was anointed, the Lord demonstrated His approval of the building by releasing a supernatural manifestation of His presence: "Then the cloud covered the tent of meeting, and the glory of the LORD filled the tabernacle" (Exod. 40:34).

Years later, when Solomon completed his Temple, the Lord once again showed His approval: "Then the house, the house of the LORD, was filled with a cloud, so that the priests could not stand to minister because of the cloud, for the glory of the LORD filled the house of God" (2 Chron. 5:13-14). It wasn't until the time of King Zedekiah that the glory of the Lord departed, never to return (see Ezek. 11:22,23).

When the second Temple was built, God promised that the glory of the latter house would be greater than that of the former (see Hag. 2:9). This promise was fulfilled in Jesus, who referred to His body as the temple (see John 2:19-21). The Church today is His Body on Earth, the Temple of the Lord. We are built together as a dwelling place for the Lord:

In whom the whole building, being fitted together is growing into a holy temple in the Lord; in whom you also are being built together into a dwelling of God in the Spirit (Eph. 2:21,22).

The apostle Paul articulated this concept in 2 Corinthians 6:16:

For we are the temple of the living God; just as God said, "I will dwell in them and walk among them; and I will be their God, and they shall be My people."

God wants to dwell in His earthly sanctuary. His desire is to abide, move, walk and demonstrate His power and presence through His redeemed dwelling place, the Body of Christ.

The person of Jesus, in the midst of His dwelling place, the believer, brings an anointing that allows each of us to do what we have been called to do on Earth. Author Kelly Varner explains it this way:

> The anointing is not a feeling, an idea, or an atmosphere. It is a knowing. It is the assurance that God is with us. And there is more. . . . The anointing is a person— Immanuel, God with us; the Messiah, the Christ.[4]

MY OWN ANOINTING

The anointing is the *presence* of God, which in turn releases the *power* of God. I remember one of the first times I experienced a supernatural manifestation of the anointing of Immanuel, "God with us." I had been asked to speak for a ladies' meeting. Never before had I spoken in front of any group. In the past people had called and asked me to speak to their church or group, but each time I declined the invitation. Usually I would recommend someone else as a speaker—anybody but me!

After months of refusing to be a speaker, the Lord began to deal with me in such a way that my sense of peace left, and I experienced an inner restlessness. The Spirit of the Lord kept nudging me. My spirit knew it was the Lord. I knew what He was asking me to do, but my mind kept talking me out of obedience: *If you can't talk to more than three people at a time, how are you going to talk to an entire group? You haven't been to Bible school. What if you don't teach the Word correctly? You've never prayed and seen a miracle as a result. What will you do if someone shows up in a wheelchair? What if you pray and absolutely nothing happens?*

For hours at a time I would lie on the floor and cry out to the Lord, "Please call someone else to do this. I want to obey You, but I have no ability to do what You are asking." Still, the Lord continued to nudge me. Finally, one day I said, "Yes, Lord. I will do what you are asking. I will not trust in my abilities, but I will trust in You."

A few weeks later I found myself speaking to a group of people. A supernatural confidence came over me when I stepped to the podium. Words poured from my mouth that I had not planned to say. *Is this the anointing?* I asked myself. After the message, I invited those who wanted prayer to come forward. People all around the room stood up, and I wondered how I would ever pray for so many.

As I took the hands of the first person in line, she suddenly fell to the floor. I took the hands of the next person, and the same thing happened. Throughout the room, people began falling under the power of the Holy Spirit. I was shocked but excited, awestruck at the power of God. The Lord had released an anointing that day to heal and set people free. His power was so strong that the people were unable to stand.

Later, over lunch, a lady asked me, "Did you think the Lord could have done this through you six months ago?"

"I didn't think He could do that through me six *hours* ago," I replied. I believe that the power of God's anointing had manifested in the meeting in much the same way as it did at the openings of Moses' Tabernacle and Solomon's Temple.

I received a number of letters following the meeting. Many of them told of healing that had been received during the meeting. Some wrote about a new freedom that had come into their lives. Several had received Jesus as their Savior. I had been able to do things under the anointing of the Holy Spirit that I had never done before.

Jesus promised this power to all who follow Him: "You shall receive power when the Holy Spirit has come upon you; and you shall be My witnesses both in Jerusalem, and in all Judea and Samaria, and even to the remotest part of the earth" (Acts 1:8). What had happened to me at that meeting was a fulfillment of this scriptural promise. Benny Hinn writes:

> The presence of God the Holy Spirit leads to the anointing of the Spirit, which is the power of God, and the power of God brings forth the manifestation of the presence. The anointing itself—an anointing of the Holy Spirit—cannot be seen, but the power, its manifestations, its effects, can and should be seen. That is why I call it "the tangible anointing."[5]

The presence and glory of the Lord were in that meeting. The Holy Spirit smeared and rubbed an anointing on me and those people that produced visible, tangible results.

Later, I pondered the statement I had heard several years before: "Don't ever stand up and speak without the anointing." Suddenly I understood. The anointing enables believers to do what they cannot do on their own!

DISCUSSION QUESTIONS

1. Describe a picture of the anointing.
2. In biblical times, what was the danger when skins used for liquids or battle shields became too dry?
3. What is the spiritual equipment God has designed to make us successful?
4. Do you know anyone who suffers from depression, discouragement or mental torment? How can that person be helped?

5. Compare and contrast the Tabernacle of Moses and Solomon's Temple with the Body of Christ.
6. What are some thoughts that try to hinder us from obeying the Lord?
7. Describe a situation in which you were empowered by the Holy Spirit to do what you could not normally do on your own.
8. Are you ready to take a risk and try again?

Do I Have an Anointing?

My husband, Dale, and I were looking forward to a relaxing weekend away with our daughter, Lori, and a couple of friends. The trip was five hours from Dallas to Hot Springs, Arkansas. Lori is not very good at sitting in a car; she likes to have something to do all the time. Having just completed a motivational gift test at church, she thought we should all take the test, too. So during the journey, Lori read aloud the questions for us to answer.

We were to respond to the questions with "always," "often," "sometimes," "rarely" or "never." After a few questions, we began laughing at our answers. Whenever Dale answered "never," it seemed my answer to the same question was "always" and vice versa. Almost without fail, we gave opposite answers to the same questions.

After completing the test, Lori drew a chart showing our answers. For many answers Dale's response was at the top of the chart. My answers to the same questions put me at the bottom of the chart. For other questions our positions were reversed. Why? Because we are total opposites in terms of our motivational gifts (see Rom. 12:3-8). The test results did not show that one of us is right and the other is wrong; they meant that we are different—not wrong, just different.

Robert Heidler explains this in *Experiencing the Spirit*:

> One of the ways the Holy Spirit wants to make you like Jesus is to place the desires of Jesus' heart into your heart, so that in a measure, you are motivated by the things that motivated Him.
>
> These expressions of the heart of Jesus are often called motivational gifts. They are God-given desires to respond to needs in specific ways.
>
> All that you do for the Lord will be shaped and colored by the motivational gift placed within you by the indwelling Spirit. The end result of this gifting is that Jesus is able to express His heart—and reveal Himself—through you.[1]

WE ARE DIFFERENT BUT NECESSARY

How boring it would be if all God's people were alike! If all trees were oaks, we would miss the magnificence of the redwoods. Roses are beautiful, but without lilacs or tulips, roses could become monotonous. God loves variety. He made the physical body with various parts. The eye is not able to do what the hand can do, nor can the hand perform the eye's function. Both are different, yet both are necessary:

> For the body is not one member, but many. If the foot should say, "Because I am not a hand, I am not a part of the body," it is not for this reason any the less a part of the

body. And if the ear should say, "Because I am n(
I am not a part of the body," it is not for this r(
the less a part of the body. If the whole body were an eye,
where would the hearing be? If the whole were hearing,
where would the sense of smell be? But now God has
placed the members, each one of them, in the body, just as
He desired (1 Cor. 12:14-18).

The same principle is true with the anointing. God has a diversi-
ty of anointings and giftings for His Body, the Church:

Now there are varieties of gifts, but the same Spirit. And
there are varieties of ministries, and the same Lord.
And there are varieties of effects, but the same God
who works all things in all persons (1 Cor. 12:4-6).

Not everyone has been called to be an apostle, although to
some extent, anyone can have an apostolic anointing. Not all are
prophets, although all may prophesy (see 1 Cor. 12:29-31). God
made each part of His Body to function in a specific way. An
evangelist does not function in the same way as a prophet. You
may not have the same anointing that your pastor has. This does
not mean your anointing is insignificant or unimportant; it only
means your function is different.

THERE IS NO SPECTATOR ANOINTING

I live in the Dallas area, where the people *love* sports.
Professional football, baseball, basketball and hockey are all
available to those who live here. In addition, of course, there are
college, high school, Little League and company sporting events.
However, relatively few people actually participate in these

sports. Most people sit in the stands or in front of their TVs and watch the athletes play. Yet the viewers become so enthralled, they feel as if they are playing.

Church life has been that same way for too many years. Most Christians sit in churches and watch the ministers do the work of the ministry. This was never God's desire. He wants every part of His Body to function according to His design. An anointing to function is available through the power of the Holy Spirit. The anointing is not only for those who stand in pulpits or lead large crusades. The anointing to function is for each and every one of us.

John Wimber said that all Christians should be ministering in the power of the Holy Spirit:

> Paul does not give the impression that in the Christian life some people are supposed to be players and others are supposed to be spectators. Christians are all players. Some of us might prefer to be spectators, because it is safer just to watch. Sometimes it can be fun to watch because it is a good chance to criticize others. It is easier to be a spectator than a participant. But Paul does not give us that option. He indicates that everyone is to participate.[2]

Growing up in church I was accustomed to being a spectator for the ministry. I remember the first retreat I attended. My excitement grew as I watched the speakers and leaders on the platform. *These must be the most spiritual people in the world*, I thought. *I wonder how they ever arrived at this place in the Spirit.* A few years later, I found myself standing on the same platform, leading a large conference. God takes ordinary people like you and me and does extraordinary things through them. The anointing to function makes the difference.

WHAT IS THE REQUIREMENT
FOR ANOINTING?

The only requirement to receive an anointing is to be born again by the Spirit of God. The anointing of the Holy Spirit is available to all believers. Jesus said:

> I will ask the Father, and He will give you another Helper, that He may be with you forever; that is the Spirit of truth, whom the world cannot receive, because it does not behold Him or know Him, but you know Him because He abides with you and will be in you (John 14:16,17).

Unbelievers cannot receive the Holy Spirit and, therefore, cannot have a true anointing. It is reserved for those who belong to the Lord. I was never able to lead a person to Jesus, pray and see someone healed, or speak a word of prophecy until after I received Jesus as my Lord and Savior. The anointing enables me to do what I could not naturally do.

Benny Hinn agrees:

> Many have misunderstood the real meaning and essence of the "anointing." They think it is some "goosebump" experience that is only a matter of feelings and thus short-lived. That is untrue. When the anointing of the Spirit comes upon your life, all confusion will vanish. You will be transformed forever.[3]

ANOINTING RELEASES POTENTIAL

Too often we look at the position we are in today, and we fail to see the *potential* God has placed within us. We look at where we are; Jesus looks at where we will be when we follow Him. Simon

Peter had potential on the inside. Nevertheless, he had what many call foot-in-mouth disease. He was famous for opening his mouth at the wrong time and saying the wrong thing, but Jesus saw what Peter could become.

One day Jesus asked Simon Peter, "Who do you say that I am?" (Matt. 16:15). Simon answered that Jesus was the Christ, the Son of the living God. Jesus responded to this insight by calling Simon a name that described his potential: "I also say to you that you are Peter, and upon this rock I will build My church; and the gates of Hades shall not overpower it" (v. 18). His name had been Simon, meaning one who is shifting and shaking. The name has the connotation of being unstable. In spite of this, Jesus called him Peter—a rock. The potential was inside of Simon to become Peter, one who was stable and solid. On the day of Pentecost, Peter stood up with a strong anointing and preached a message that caused 3,000 people to receive Jesus as their Savior. The anointing released the potential inside Peter, and the anointing releases the potential in our lives, too.

Jesus does not see us as we see ourselves, tainted by the way we have been, or *thought* we were, in the past. Most Christians rejoice at the time of salvation when they hear 2 Corinthians 5:17: "Therefore if anyone is in Christ, he is a new creature; the old things passed away; behold, new things have come." It is exciting to think we are not the same as we were before we received Jesus.

Sometimes we are different for a few days or weeks, maybe a few months. Then one day something happens. We say the wrong words, we think the wrong thoughts—maybe we even do the wrong things. *What happened?* we ask ourselves. We thought old things had passed away and all things were now new. We begin to question our new life.

In the Bible, "salvation" (Hebrew: *Yeshua*; Greek: *soteria*) is a rich word that means deliverance from enemies, preservation,

redemption from sin, eternal life and the process of sanctifica-
tion. Its meanings also include healing, health, deliverance from
apprehension and peace. When an architect draws blueprints for
a home or other building, he knows where each door and window will be placed. He marks the spots where electrical outlets
and lights will be. The potential for the building is on the blueprint. However, the building is not fully manifested when the
blueprint is completed.

When we put our trust in Christ as Savior, all the potential
for our lives was on the blueprint that God put inside of us; but
that potential was not yet fully manifested. The fullness of the
anointing for our lives was placed within us, as we see in
Scripture:

> Seeing that His divine power has granted to us everything
> pertaining to life and godliness, through the true knowl-
> edge of Him who called us by His own glory and excel-
> lence. For by these He has granted to us His precious and
> magnificent promises, in order that by them you might
> become partakers of the divine nature, having escaped
> the corruption that is in the world by lust (2 Pet. 1:3,4).

ANOINTING IS AVAILABLE TO ALL

Each of us is in the process of allowing the full manifestation of
God's nature and anointing to flow through us. That anointing
is not limited by social or economic status, race, background or
even chronological age. Children can flow in the anointing and
do so quite often—and quite effectively.

While my husband and I were pastoring a church, we helped
train home-group leaders. During one of the home meetings,
I worked with the children while their parents enjoyed the teach-

ing time. There were about eight of them, ages five to nine, in attendance. How excited they were as I told them about young Samuel, who learned to hear the voice of the Lord at an early age (see 1 Sam. 3). We then prayed and asked the Lord to speak to each of the children. One by one, the children told the group what he or she had heard the Lord speak. I wrote each of these "words from God" on paper. The children spoke in words and phrases beyond their years or natural abilities and knowledge; they spoke in a way that only the Lord could have spoken through them.

Later, over refreshments, I asked the parents if they would like to hear what their children had prophesied. Imagine their amazement when they heard the words spoken by their children! Most of those adults didn't prophesy; the children were operating in an anointing their parents had not yet experienced.

While in Korea in 1993 at the Gideon's Army meeting, I observed 50 children, ages 7 to 12, in intercession. These children were not in attendance because their parents were there; they had been invited as delegates from various nations because they were effective intercessors.

God has an anointing for each of us, regardless of age or gender.

One day, during the conference, we found many of the children in deep travail, interceding for children around the world. Others were praying for and encouraging those travailing in prayer. Many adults have not had such an experience in intercession. However, these children had an anointing to intercede for children all over the world, that they would be freed from the torment of the enemy. God will anoint children and youth to pray, teach, prophesy, heal and deliver.

God also anoints the older generation. I will never forget the story of Rev. John Garlock's mother. She was well advanced in age when she decided to take a trip to visit relatives. While waiting in the airport, she spotted a young man and approached him to check on his spiritual condition. By the time she caught her plane, the man's eternal destiny had changed; he had found eternal life in Jesus. Although this lady was a senior in age, she had an incredibly strong anointing for evangelism. In fact, God has an anointing for each of us, regardless of age or gender.

The prophet Joel spoke of these days:

> It will come about after this that I will pour out My Spirit on all mankind; and your sons and daughters will prophesy, your old men will dream dreams, your young men will see visions. And even on the male and female servants I will pour out My Spirit in those days (Joel 2:28,29).

The Holy Spirit is able to teach us how to operate in the anointing: "But the Helper, the Holy Spirit, whom the Father will send in My name, He will teach you all things" (John 14:26). That does not mean we have no need for teachers. Jesus knew we needed teachers and gave some as gifts to the Church when He ascended to heaven (see Eph. 4:11). However, the Holy Spirit will also instruct us as we walk with the Lord. Therefore, we do not need a formula, a checklist or a seminary degree to minister in His name.

Years ago, during a worship service in my church, there was present a lady named Paula who had recently been diagnosed with terminal cancer. As I worshiped the Lord, I sensed Him speaking to me, impressing me to lay hands on Paula and pray for her healing. Not wanting to interrupt the service, I quietly moved to a chair next to her. As I laid my hand on her shoulder and began to pray, she started weeping. "I feel heat," she cried. "Something is happening in my body!"

A few days later, Paula entered the hospital for scheduled surgery. When the surgeon operated on Paula, he could find no trace of the cancer. Paula had been healed! Something really had happened that Sunday when she felt heat go through her body!

No one had taught me how to release the anointing for healing. The Holy Spirit had been my Teacher.

Jesus wants to live His life and demonstrate His power through every believer. He does not look at a person's educational background, natural abilities, gender, socioeconomic status or outward appearance. He looks for those with hearts that seek after Him. The Spirit of the Lord searches for those who will allow Him to live His life through them.

The desire of the Lord is to pour out the oil of a fresh anointing upon His Church. For this to happen, we must be vessels that will become the new wineskin:

> No one puts new wine into old wineskins; otherwise the new wine will burst the skins and it will be spilled out, and the skins will be ruined. But new wine must be put into fresh wineskins. And no one, after drinking old wine, wishes for new; for he says, "The old is good enough" (Luke 5:37-39).

Believers have long thought that the old was good enough. We have been satisfied watching the professionals do the work of the ministry. Today, however, God is raising up a people who want the new wine of the Spirit. They are recognizing that the Lord has an anointing for them. They are not content with church the way it has been.

When our son, Mark, was two, he liked things to be done the same way every time. One day, when he arrived at his grandmother's house, he developed the same malady all children experience when they visit grandma: extreme hunger. After Mark's grandmother placed him in a chair at the kitchen table, she prepared him a snack of peanut butter and crackers. She carefully spread the peanut butter on the crackers and put them on a plate. Mark picked up the first cracker and looked at both sides. "The peanut butter is on the wrong side," he exclaimed. In his mind there was only one correct side for peanut butter. After all, I had always put the peanut butter on the opposite side of the cracker; anything different surely must be wrong.

We often are that way in the Church. We have very definite ideas about what God does and does not do. Many of us think that only one side of the cracker can hold peanut butter—that only those involved in full-time ministry can have an anointing. But God wants to smear the entire cracker with His anointing!

Today God is forming a new wineskin in His Church—a wineskin made up of ordinary believers. He is releasing a fresh anointing on all who will receive, and they will be used to help pour out the new wine of revival. The cry from the hearts of this new wineskin is "The old is not good enough!" Along with the psalmist, they declare, "I have been anointed with fresh oil" (Ps. 92:10).

DISCUSSION QUESTIONS

1. Describe an area of ministry you have sometimes pictured yourself in. Have you ever attempted to minister in this area? If so, what happened?

2. Talk about the differences between the ways you handle problem situations and the ways your spouse or a close friend handles similar situations.
3. What do you think your motivational gift is according to the list mentioned in Romans 12:6-8?
4. What would you like to do in ministry that you feel unable to do at the present time? How can you change this?
5. Is there an area in your spiritual life where you are crying out, "The old is not good enough"? If so, describe it.
6. What are you going to do about it?

Chapter Three

Different Strokes for Different Folks

The smell of freshly baked muffins filled the house. Every Saturday morning the family looked forward to biting into these wonderful blueberry-filled treats, and this weekend was no exception. I had been using the same recipe since shortly after Dale and I married, so why change a good thing?

But on this day, as I removed the pan from the oven, I noticed something was wrong. The batter usually rose in the hot oven, producing large, fluffy muffins. This time the muffins were half their usual height. What had I done wrong? Was the temperature setting incorrect? Did I not allow the proper amount of time for cooking? Had I not followed the recipe exactly?

After carefully retracing my steps and examining the recipe, I identified the problem. One of the ingredients was missing. How could I have forgotten the baking powder after making these muffins so many times before? A small amount of the neglected ingredient seemed so insignificant. But without it the muffins were heavy and did not taste good. Although the recipe comprised only small amounts of several ingredients, all were important. Each one was distinctive, and each had a special function to perform.

DIVERSE ANOINTINGS, DIVINE BLEND

Anointings and giftings in the Body of Christ are similar to the ingredients in a recipe. Each person has been created by God and given special abilities. Not all have the same abilities, however. My husband has an ability to work with wires and electricity. Dale has been working with electronic equipment since he built his first radio at the age of 10. I, on the other hand, consider myself blessed when I can figure out which way to insert a grounded plug into an electrical outlet. Dale says I am the least mechanically inclined person he has ever met. However, he has never learned to sew a button on a shirt. His fingers just can't seem to manipulate the needle. Around our house, we are both needed to complete the various and sundry tasks required to keep a household functioning.

The Body of Christ is the same way. God has given different people distinctive anointings. All are necessary, and all are significant:

From whom the whole body, being fitted and held together by that which every joint supplies, according to the proper working of each individual part, causes the growth of the body for the building up of itself in love (Eph. 4:16).

Looking at the anointing ointment of the Old Testament, we see a picture of diverse anointings coming together to form a whole:

Moreover, the LORD spoke to Moses, saying, "Take also for yourself the finest of spices: of flowing myrrh five hundred shekels, and of fragrant cinnamon half as much, two hundred and fifty, and of fragrant cane two hundred and fifty, and of cassia five hundred, according to the shekel of the sanctuary, and of olive oil a hin. And you shall make of these a holy anointing oil, a perfume mixture, the work of a perfumer; it shall be a holy anointing oil" (Exod. 30:22-25).

God gave Moses a recipe with the ingredients that were to be used in making the anointing ointment. Each of the ingredients had distinctive characteristics, all were combined together into one measure of oil, and the entire mixture was called holy. In 1 Peter 2:5, believers in Christ are called a "holy priesthood," blended together to display the power of the Lord on the earth.

The Old Testament anointing oil was used for equipping priests and others for ministry. New Testament believers need the anointing of the Holy Spirit to equip them for ministry. We also need God's Spirit in us to produce the fruit of the Spirit, or God's character (see Gal. 5:22). The Holy Spirit performs both of these functions—equipping the believer for ministry and producing fruit—but the two functions are different.

During the early years of my walk in the Spirit, much discussion was taking place among believers about the gifts of the Spirit and the fruit of the Spirit. I recall attending a Bible study on fruit of the Spirit, where the teacher said, "What you really need is the fruit of the Spirit. You just need to be like Jesus."

Oh, yes! my heart cried out. *I want to be like Jesus! Lord, help me to have the fruit of the Spirit in my life.*

On another day I attended a different Bible study, and this teacher taught on the gifts of the Spirit: "What you need are the gifts of the Spirit. You need to be like Jesus and see sick bodies healed, captives set free and the lame walking."

Again my heart cried out, *Yes, Lord! This is what I want. I want to be like You! I want the gifts of the Spirit and the power of God in my life.*

Which did I want, the gifts of the Spirit or the fruit of the Spirit? How I wrestled with the question! One day the answer came: I didn't need to make a decision—I could have both! Jesus' life showed forth both the fruit and the gifts of the Spirit. If ever I was going to be like Him, I needed both in my life.

Lori Wilke, in her book *The Costly Anointing*, explains why the believer needs both the fruit and the gifts of the Spirit:

> The fruit of the Spirit not only accompanies the gifts of the Spirit, but helps to develop the gifts. Without the nature of God, the gifts themselves will short-circuit and deplete. The fruit serves to enhance the gifts and to bring them forth with grace and beauty. The anointing, therefore, is twofold, encompassing both the gifts and the fruits of the Spirit. Both are imparted to the believer as a divine unction from God.[1]

I also like the way Robert Heidler explains this:

> The Spirit's *indwelling* is designed to *mature* us, causing us to grow in the Lord. The Spirit's *empowering* is designed to *equip* us, enabling us to serve the Lord.
>
> To put it another way: The Spirit *indwells* us to give us victory over sin, making us *holy*. The Spirit *empowers* us to give us tools for ministry, making us *effective*.
>
> Or: The Spirit *lives within you* to give you the *character of Christ*. The Spirit *comes upon you* in power to give you the *ministry of Christ*.[2]

OLD TESTAMENT ANOINTING VERSUS NEW TESTAMENT ANOINTING

In the Old Testament the Holy Spirit would come upon a person to empower that individual for a particular task. The Spirit would then lift from the person when the task was completed.

The prophet Elijah experienced the empowering of the Holy Spirit on numerous occasions. One involved a widow whose son had died. Elijah took the child and carried him to an upper room. An anointing for intercession and miracles came upon the prophet when he prayed.

> He called to the LORD and said, "O LORD my God, hast Thou also brought calamity to the widow with whom I am staying, by causing her son to die?" Then he stretched himself upon the child three times, and called to the LORD, and said, "O LORD my God, I pray Thee, let this child's life return to him." And the LORD heard the voice of Elijah, and the life of the child returned to him and he revived. And Elijah took the child and brought him down from the upper room into the house and gave him to his mother; and Elijah said, "See, your son is alive." Then the woman said to Elijah, "Now I know that you are a man of God, and that the word of the LORD in your mouth is truth" (1 Kings 17:20-24).

Elijah did not pray for every dead child he came across and see them all raised to life. However, he was given an anointing that equipped him for this particular task. An anointing was "loaned" to him for a short time to accomplish God's purposes.

Young David also experienced the anointing:

> Then Samuel took the horn of oil and anointed him in
> the midst of his brothers; and the Spirit of the LORD came
> mightily upon David from that day forward (1 Sam.
> 16:13).

Until the prophet Samuel anointed him, David was merely a shepherd boy. After the anointing, he was equipped to kill a giant and to do numerous deeds. The anointing was loaned to him at various times for various exploits for God. This anointing of power from heaven enabled him to do what he could not normally do.

I remember the first car Dale and I bought after we were married. We borrowed money from a bank to purchase it. The bank gave us a piece of paper stating we could have use of the car for a certain period of time, as long as we made regular payments. What the paper actually was saying was that we did not yet own the car. The bank owned the car and loaned it to us while we were paying for it. We could use the car for a short period of time until the next payment was due. When we made the next payment, we could use the car for another month.

After a few years, we received another piece of paper. This paper stated that we had made all our payments on the car. Therefore, the car now permanently belonged to us. The debt had been paid. Because it belonged to us, we had permanent access to it, and we could now use the car anytime we needed it. This is a vivid picture of the difference between the anointing on individuals in the Old Testament and the anointing on those in the New Testament.

From the day of Pentecost forward, believers have been empowered by the same Holy Spirit that was manifested in the Old Testament. In the Old Testament, God released revelation and power at His sovereign will upon certain individuals. After Jesus ascended to heaven, He gave us gifts to equip us for supernatural ministry (see Eph. 4:11,12). The Lord has since been releasing revelation and power by His same sovereign will to those who will receive and follow Him:

> But to each one is given the manifestation of the Spirit for the common good (1 Cor. 12:7).

Peter and John were two New Testament men who received and followed the Lord Jesus. As believers, they received an anointing for supernatural ministry. One day, as they were on their way to the Temple to pray, a crippled man stopped them. They walked the same road frequently and had probably had seen this man before. Although the path they walked and the man they encountered were familiar, something unusual happened that day:

> Now Peter and John were going up to the temple at the ninth hour, the hour of prayer. And a certain man who had been lame from his mother's womb was being carried along, whom they used to set down every day at the gate of the temple which is called Beautiful, in order to beg alms of those who were entering the temple. And when he saw Peter and John about to go into the temple, he began asking to receive alms. And Peter, along with John, fixed his gaze upon him and said, "Look at us!" And he began to give them his attention, expecting to receive something from them. But Peter said, "I do not possess silver and gold, but what I do have I give to you: In the name of Jesus Christ the Nazarene—walk!" And seizing him by the right hand, he raised him up; and immediately his feet and his ankles were strengthened. And with a leap, he stood upright and began to walk; and he entered the temple with them, walking and leaping and praising God (Acts 3:1-8).

Peter possessed something the man needed: the anointing of the Spirit. Rather than giving the man the money he asked for, Peter discerned his true need. Sitting before him was a man with no hope. The man had never known what it was to walk. He had never experienced the joy of leaping, jumping and dancing. He had no hope of ever living a normal life. Sitting and begging from others was the best he could imagine. Peter had a revelation that the man didn't need money; instead, he needed a supernatural touch from God.

Realizing that he had been empowered by the Holy Spirit for ministry, Peter spoke to the lame man. First, he told the man to look at John and him. Why did he say that? Peter knew that God's power was residing within them. Also, Peter let the man know that they were as destitute as he was. They didn't have the riches of this world to give to him. Finally, Peter said he would give the man what he *did* have. He had something in his possession better than silver and gold. Peter boldly spoke to the hopeless man: "Look at us. We have something for you from Jesus."

How sad that many in the Church have never realized what they possess!

What did Peter and John have? An anointing for a miracle! After commanding the man to rise and walk, the lame legs straightened, muscles were restored and strength entered his body. Rather than sitting along the road, watching others do what he could not, the man now joined Peter and John. Can you imagine the sound of rejoicing when he entered the Temple that day, healed, whole and praising the God of Peter and John?

Many people are hopeless and helpless today. How sad that many members of the Church have never realized what they possess! Believers have the same power of God residing within them that Peter and John had. No longer do we need to wait for a power to come down from heaven. This power came down on the Day of Pentecost. Jesus promised it to us before He ascended to heaven: "You shall receive power when the Holy Spirit has come upon you" (Acts 1:8).

In the Old Testament, the Holy Spirit was in the heavens, operating from His place in glory. On the Day of Pentecost, the Holy Spirit came down from heaven to Earth and entered the bodies and spirits of redeemed men and women:

> Or do you not know that your body is a temple of the Holy Spirit who is in you, whom you have from God, and that you are not your own? (1 Cor. 6:19).

Now we are the temples of the Holy Spirit. While the Tabernacle in the Old Testament was anointed with oil, today believers have an anointing within themselves for supernatural ministry.

RECOGNIZING THE ANOINTING

One of the first times I experienced the anointing I was in church on a Sunday morning. The presence of the Lord seemed almost tangible as we worshiped Him. Suddenly, my hands felt as if they were on fire! What was happening to me? Was the air conditioner not working? If so, why was it that only my hands were so hot?

As I stood with questions still flooding my mind, I sensed words inside speaking to me: *There's healing in your hands.* My mind began to reason, *Those are the words of a song.* Again, I heard on the inside, *There's healing in your hands*. Once more, I reasoned with what I was hearing: *I distinctly remember singing those words in a song*. Periodically I would put my hands on the back of one of the metal chairs. The air conditioner was obviously working because the metal chair backs were quite cold. Maybe if I could keep my hands on a cold surface, they would cool off.

After a few minutes of my silent dialogue, the pastor's wife came to me from the front row. "What is the Lord saying to you?" she asked.

"Nothing," I replied. I didn't understand what was happening; surely I didn't want to tell her! However, she knew how to hear the Lord and would not give up. After she asked me the same question several times, I reluctantly answered, "I think He is saying that I have healing in my hands. They feel so hot."

"Come with me," she insisted.

When we got to the front of the church, she whispered something into the pastor's ear. He then turned and announced over the microphone, "The anointing is on Barbara today for healing. If you need to be healed, come to the front and she will pray for you."

It seemed that every person at church that day needed to be healed. As I tried to calm the panic rising inside me, I moved toward the first person who had come to the front of the church and carefully laid my hands on the person's head. Instantly, that individual fell to the floor. The same thing happened with the second person and the third. Over and over, God's power flowed through sick bodies, and they dropped to the floor under God's power. Other people shouted and laughed, jumping up and down and rejoicing.

After I had prayed for many people, some started sharing about the healings they received. Stiff joints were now flexible. Pain was gone. Hearing was improved. I was so surprised! God had truly allowed the anointing to flow through *me*; He didn't operate only through pastors and leaders. Later I learned that the heat I had felt in my hands was a physical manifestation of the anointing. It was not the heat that had healed, but rather, it was the power of God. He had used a physical sign to help me sense the anointing was present to heal.

Since that day, I have prayed for hundreds of people and seen them healed by the Lord. Very seldom do I feel heat or any other physical manifestation. I have learned to discern the anointing and step out in faith when I feel nothing physically. Some of the greatest miracles I have seen have been during times when I felt nothing. However, there are times when the Lord will let me feel the anointing, and such times are wonderful.

I have learned that the Lord places an anointing inside us that does not leave. The anointing I received that Sunday morning equipped me for ministry. Like Peter and John, I was able to give to the sick people what I possessed—an anointing to heal. The anointing is not for a few superstars. It is for the everyday believer—for me and for you!

DISCUSSION QUESTIONS

1. Compare the recipe for the anointing ointment Moses received to the anointing available to us today.
2. What is the purpose of the anointing for New Testament believers?
3. How did the Holy Spirit empower a person in the Old Testament?
4. How does He empower a person in the New Testament?
5. Describe a time when you experienced the anointing.
6. What gifting do you possess that people around you need? What are you going to do about it?

7. Are you willing to be used by the Lord to minister to those in need?

Chapter Four

All Can Prophesy—
Including You!

The lady speaking at the meeting ended her message by asking all of us to close our eyes. She began to speak of healings the Lord was bring about in our midst. She also told us things she sensed the Lord was saying to some of us. My walk in the Spirit was new, and the format of the meeting was strange to me. I had never heard anyone tell others what God was saying to them.

THE TRUTH HITS HOME

My mind was flooded with questions. *How did this lady know what God wanted to say to other people? Did God really speak like that today? I thought the only way God spoke to us was through the Bible. How could I be sure it was God and not just something the lady was imagining? Maybe she knew these people, and they had planned it all before the meeting began. Could this be a hoax meant to deceive people? After all, my*

*church had admonished us to be careful. The Bible also warns believers
not to be deceived.*

Then suddenly, to my surprise, I heard the lady speaking to
me: "When you were a little girl, you said to the Lord, 'Lord, I will
be a missionary for you.' The Lord wants you to know you will be
a missionary for Him, just not in the way you thought." The
words were like arrows piercing my heart. I knew the Lord was
speaking to me, and all my questions vanished. The truth of the
gift of prophecy being for today was beginning to hit home.

As the words penetrated my spirit, I saw a vision of myself as
a 10-year-old child, sitting in a Sunday School class. The room
was familiar, and I heard myself say, "Lord, I will be a missionary
for you."

As the vision began to fade, I realized I was now 31 years old,
with a husband and three small children. Many years earlier
I had made the commitment to the Lord to be a missionary, but
I had forgotten my commitment completely until I heard this
woman speak. The Lord had not forgotten, though, and He was
now making a promise to me, even though I had forgotten my
promise to Him. At the very moment I heard God speak, I knew
His words were forever etched on my heart, although I would
not see the fulfillment of that promise right away.

After experiencing this prophetic anointing, I had an intense
desire to learn more. If God really did speak to people today,
I wanted Him to speak more to me. *What*, I wondered, *is prophecy? Can God communicate through all believers, or just through a few,
such as the speaker I had just heard?*

Through study I discovered many biblical references to
prophets and prophecies. The coming of the Holy Spirit and the
completion of the Bible did not remove our need for God's
prophetic voice. Peter, speaking of the prophetic anointing on
the Day of Pentecost, quoted the Old Testament prophet, Joel
who had spoken God's promise of prophecy for today:

"And it shall be in the last days," God says, "That I will pour forth of My Spirit upon all mankind; and your sons and your daughters shall prophesy, and your young men shall see visions, and your old men shall dream dreams; even upon My bondslaves, both men and women, I will in those days pour forth of My Spirit and they shall prophesy" (Acts 2:17,18).

Paul likewise emphasized the need for prophets and inspired divine utterances when he told us to "desire earnestly to prophesy" (1 Cor. 14:39). Believers, then, are to covet a prophetic anointing.

In the Old Testament, the main Hebrew word for prophet is *nabi*, a word derived from the verb *naba*, which means "to flow or boil up or over." Naba gives a picture of a bubbling or pouring forth, the essential idea in this context being of one who speaks authoritatively for another (see Exod. 7:1,2), particularly one who brings a direct communication from God (see Num. 12:4-8). This bubbling or gushing forth of God's prophetic words is a human activity in response to the prophetic anointing. The prophetic message pours forth from an anointed believer like water from a fountain.

In the New Testament, the Greek word for prophet is *prophetes*, meaning one who speaks forth the mind and counsel of God. Prophetes is derived from the Greek verb *propheteia*, a declaration of that which cannot be known by natural means.

Frank Damazio, in his book *Developing the Prophetic Ministry*, writes:

When men would prophesy, whether in the Old or New Testament, the Spirit of God would inspire their speech and cause His own words to bubble forth. The same is true in the Church today. Men and women can utter words from the Lord as He inspires them to speak, for the edification, exhortation and comfort of the entire Body.[1]

In 1 Corinthians 12:29 Paul asks the question, "All are not prophets, are they?" The obvious answer is no. But in 1 Corinthians 14:5, Paul goes on to say he wishes all would prophesy. A few verses later, Paul states, "For you can all prophesy" (v. 31). All the manifestation gifts of the Spirit, including the gift of prophecy, are contained in the Holy Spirit (see 1 Cor. 12:9). The Holy Spirit lives within us, as believers, and can flow through us anytime God chooses. Therefore, all believers have the potential to prophesy, including you and me. All are not prophets, but all can prophesy.

Since it is the Lord's will for all to prophesy, why don't all churches believe that the prophetic anointing is for today? To answer that question, we must look at Church history. The Early Church experienced operation of all the Holy Spirit gifts and ministries. Apostles and prophets were functioning and were respected. As time passed and the Church became more institutionalized, God's people began to look to the bishops, or Church leaders, for manifestations of the gifts. Although never completely lost, prophecy and the ministry of prophets gradually faded into the background.

Peter said that a time would come when God would restore to the Church all that had been spoken by the mouths of His prophets (see Acts 3:21). Many Protestant Church historians believe this period of restoration began in 1517 with Martin Luther and the Reformation. Essential truths of the Bible that had been lost or forgotten by previous generations, such as salvation by grace through faith rather than works, were rediscovered at that time. Since then God has continued to restore His Church, allowing it to rediscover old truths. These truths are not new to God; they are simply new to the generation receiving the fresh revelation.

RESISTANCE TO THE GIFT OF PROPHECY TODAY

From the latter part of the nineteenth century and early part of the twentieth century, further restoration of the ministry of the Holy Spirit and His empowering was set into motion. The Latter Rain Movement of the 1950s began a restoration of healing and the use of prophetic presbytery. Prophets and the gift of prophecy began to be more widely recognized and practiced during the 1980s. The office of prophet and prophetic ministry are once again becoming established in the Church. This does not mean every local church or every denomination recognizes this ministry. Many do not accept prophetic ministry for a variety of reasons. Bill Hamon refers to this issue in *Prophets and the Prophetic Movement*:

> We will probably never know all the reasons why so many Christian teachers, over the centuries, came to deny that apostles and prophets still function in the Church. Some Christians based their argument for the reliability of Scripture on its apostolic origins; that is, they claimed that we could trust the authority of New Testament Scripture because each book was either written by an apostle or with the sanction of an apostle. For these Christians, then, to speak of modern-day apostles seemed tantamount to claiming that certain individuals today could write new Scripture with the same authority as the New Testament writers. They consequently rejected the notion of apostles in the Church today, and

they rejected the idea of modern-day prophets for similar reasons.

Of course, every responsible participant in the current Prophetic Movement would insist that the authority of the individuals who were inspired to write the Scriptures was a unique authority, and that the words of contemporary prophets and apostles are not equal to the Scriptures.[2]

Hamon gives several other reasons why he believes many churches reject prophetic ministry, including the fact that many non-Christian leaders throughout history have used the title "prophet." Some deny the existence of prophetic ministry because they reject the authority of individuals who use that title to draw people away from Christ.

Another reason for the rejection of prophecy is the belief of some churches that the gifts of the Holy Spirit ceased with the Early Church. There are probably many other reasons, but these seem to be the major reasons many churches today reject the idea of prophets and prophetic ministry. Regardless, God is restoring prophets and prophetic ministry as promised in His Word.

But restoration of truth is often accompanied by imbalanced and peculiar people. Exclusive groups develop, claiming they are the only ones who possess the truth of God's Word. Often there are extremes to the right or left of the truth being restored. Unusual people may show up in church meetings. I once heard someone say, "Where there is light, there will be bugs."

However, we must not throw out present truth simply because there are places of imbalance populated by spiritually and emotionally immature people. The Lord will help us find the balance necessary to be what God intends for His Church. We must do as Paul admonished the Thessalonians:

Do not quench the Spirit; do not despise prophetic utterances. But examine everything carefully; hold fast to that which is good (1 Thess. 5:19-21).

FOUR AREAS OF PROPHECY

As we examine prophetic ministry, we find there are four spheres, or areas, of prophecy. The first area is the prophecy of Scripture.

But know this first of all, that no prophecy of Scripture is a matter of one's own interpretation, for no prophecy was ever made by an act of human will, but men moved by the Holy Spirit spoke from God (2 Pet. 1:20,21).

The truths of God's Word are the highest form of prophecy. God, through the power of the Holy Spirit, inspired men to write the Bible. As a result, it is completely accurate and without error. In fact, the Bible is the highest form of God's communication to man. The Scriptures are used to judge all other prophecy. If a word contradicts the Bible, it is not from God and should be thrown out.

The second area of prophecy is the spirit of prophecy:

I fell at his feet to worship him. And he said to me, "Do not do that; I am a fellow servant of yours and your brethren who hold the testimony of Jesus; worship God. For the testimony of Jesus is the spirit of prophecy" (Rev. 19:10).

The spirit of prophecy is an anointing. At times, when the spirit of prophecy is released, anyone who exercises a small measure of faith can prophesy. How does this happen?

Usually a spirit of prophecy is released when one of two circumstances is present. Sometimes when there is a powerful presence of the Lord in a congregation, the spirit of prophecy will
manifest. Many times this happens when believers are worshiping and the powerful presence of the Lord is evident. Another
condition that releases the spirit of prophecy is when people are
under the mantle or influence of a prophet. Persons empowered
by the Holy Spirit as prophets have a gifting to release others to
prophesy. This does not mean they necessarily have to say anything for this to happen; the very presence of a prophet can
cause others to receive an anointing to prophesy.

An example of this second condition can be seen in the life
of Moses. God took the Spirit that was upon Moses and put it
on the 70 elders of Israel:

> Then the LORD came down in the cloud and spoke to
> him; and He took of the Spirit who was upon him and
> placed Him upon the seventy elders. And it came about
> that when the Spirit rested upon them, they prophesied.
> But they did not do it again (Num. 11:25).

The elders were under the influence of Moses the prophet. God
transferred some of the Spirit that was on Moses to the elders,
and they were able to prophesy for a time. The elders were not
prophets, but they received an anointing to prophesy.

The third area of prophecy is the gift of prophecy within the
Church. One of the nine manifestation gifts of the Holy Spirit
is the gift of prophecy (see 1 Cor. 12:8-11). The gift of prophecy
is available to every believer, although this gift does not necessarily include revelation or prediction for the future. Prophecy is
given mainly to encourage, strengthen and comfort, as we see in
1 Corinthians 14:3: "But one who prophesies speaks to men for
edification and exhortation and consolation."

Finally, the fourth area of prophecy is the office of the prophet. Prophets are a gift from Jesus to the Church. Not all who prophesy are prophets. The Holy Spirit gives the gift of prophecy, but the Lord Jesus gives the gift of the prophet:

> And He gave some as apostles, and some as prophets, and some as evangelists, and some as pastors and teachers (Eph. 4:11).

The office of prophet is primarily a governmental function in the Church, often being part of the leadership team for a local church. These prophets, sometimes referred to as prophetic presbyteries, help bring vision, correction and direction.

The office of prophet also has a twofold ministry relative to the Word. First, prophets unfold and reveal the depths of God's Word for the Church's understanding. These are days of revelation and restoration. The prophets who operate in the government of the Church are vital for they break open fresh doctrinal revelation of truth from God's Word for our generation: "Which in other generations was not made known to the sons of men, as it has now been revealed to His holy apostles and prophets in the Spirit" (Eph. 3:5).

Second, prophets may also foretell things to come: "Surely the Lord GOD does nothing unless He reveals His secret counsel to His servants the prophets" (Amos 3:7).

GOD WILL PERFECT THE EXERCISING OF THE GIFT

These are days of restoration. The Lord desires to communicate with His people. As we are empowered by the Holy Spirit and equipped by the ascension gift ministries (see Eph. 4:11), the Body of Christ will hear more clearly what the Spirit is saying to the Church.

The anointing oil of the Old Testament gives us a picture of the prophetic anointing. One of the ingredients of the oil was a spice called myrrh (see Exod. 30:22-25). Myrrh comes from a bitter plant from which, after it is bruised, sweetness is obtained. The word is taken from the Hebrew word *mor*, which means bitter or strong. Christ gave of Himself freely. He was made sin (bitter) for our sake, but from His bruising comes the sweetness of the Holy Spirit. In death, His lifeless body was anointed with the myrrh, and He was made our purification. However, He did not stay dead. Jesus arose! Out of death came life. The Holy Spirit empowers believers with a prophetic anointing to speak life into dead situations so transformation may occur.

A prophetic anointing can bring life out of death.

Sometimes we, as believers, live or work in regions where there is no life of the Spirit. Things around us seem dead. That is when we need a prophetic anointing to bring change. A prophetic anointing has the ability to bring life out of death. In a vision, the prophet Ezekiel was taken by the Spirit to a valley full of dead, dry bones. He was told to prophesy over the bones. Transformation came after he prophesied, "O dry bones, hear the word of the LORD" (Ezek. 37:4). However, prophesying one time did not produce the desired results. Ezekiel had to prophesy again. Afterward, the dead bones rose as an exceedingly great army.

Today we need to prophesy over our family, our place of business and our city for change to come. And we may need to prophesy more than once. We need the prophetic anointing.

How then do you develop your prophetic anointing?

- *Study the Scriptures, especially the passages on prophecy.* Our faith increases as we see God's will for prophetic ministry.
- *Cultivate relationships with prophetic people.* There is no substitute for hearing the experiences of others. The mentoring of those older in the Spirit teaches us principles that cannot be found in textbooks or classes.
- *Ask the Lord for sensitivity to His Spirit.* We see people each day who need encouragement, comfort and building up. The Lord can give you a word, a Scripture verse or a picture/vision for the person in need.
- *Become a student of the Word.* All prophecy must agree with the Bible. When I came into the fullness of the Spirit, I could find no churches, radio or TV programs or Christian literature teaching on the prophetic. Yet I had such an intense hunger for God's Word that I devoured it for hours each day. God taught me much during those years. Later, I met other prophetic people, bookstores opened, and other helps became available. God will send the help needed, but He wants us to go to His Word first.
- *Develop a strong prayer life.* I first learned to hear the voice of the Lord in prayer. While I was praying and listening, the Lord would speak to me. I kept a pencil and paper handy and wrote down any impressions from the Lord. When the time was right, I asked other spiritual people if what I had written was from God. This helped confirm to me that I was hearing from the Lord.

After spending hours in the Word and in prayer, the time came when the Lord gave me a release to publicly prophesy. I will never forget how hard it was for me to open my mouth and release the prophetic word. I was in church on a Sunday morning, and we had been worshiping for about 20 minutes when I sensed the Lord speaking a prophetic word to me.

Lord, I prayed silently, *if I just knew this was You and not me, I would open my mouth and prophesy*. The congregation kept singing, and the word kept speaking inside of me. When the pastor preached that morning, he spoke on the very same word that I had sensed that day. I went home after church and repented. "Lord," I cried, "please give me another opportunity! Next time, I will be obedient and step out to prophesy."

The next Sunday the same thing happened, and my dialogue with the Lord was the same as the Sunday before. *Lord, if I just knew this was You and not me* . . . . Again, the pastor preached the same thing I had sensed the Lord saying. After church I had another repentance service. This scenario continued for several weeks. Finally, my faith reached a new level. I stepped out and prophesied what I sensed the Lord was saying to the congregation. The pastor confirmed the word by preaching the word I had prophesied. Each time I was willing to step out and prophesy, the Lord would confirm the word was from Him, and my level of faith would grow.

How, then, is the prophetic anointing released?

- *Faith*. Faith is the main ingredient in the release of prophecy. Faith to prophesy grows in proportion to the level of obedience to prophesy. Faith is like a spiritual muscle that must be exercised. The more the faith muscle is exercised, the stronger it becomes.
- *The voice of the Lord*. There are four voices that can speak to us: the voice of the flesh (self), the voice of the enemy (Satan), the voice of the world (society, others) and the voice of God. It takes time and practice to discern the voice of the Lord. Samuel spent time as a child learning

to recognize the voice of the Lord (see 1 Sam. 3). We must be patient as we learn. Every prophet and prophetic person has to go through the same process.

• *Say it, don't just pray it.* One of the ways I learned to hear the Lord was in praying with others. I found myself praying things I did not know in the natural. The prophetic anointing flowed through me, and I did not recognize what was happening. After this happened a few times, I incorporated the prophetic into my prayers, something like this: "Father, I thank you for Susan. Thank you that you have put healing in her hands. Lord, she is going to be used to minister wholeness to many people." Later, when I learned to distinguish God's voice while in prayer for someone, I would stop praying and say something like this: "Susan, I sense the Lord wants to encourage you today. He is showing me that there is an anointing for healing in your hands. He is going to use you to minister wholeness to many people."

God's Word says all can prophesy—including you. Receive the myrrh so the prophetic anointing can bring life and hope to all the dead places you encounter. Let God use you to release His Word to all who need to experience a fresh touch from the Lord.

DISCUSSION QUESTIONS

1. Have you ever received a prophetic word from another person? What was your response?
2. What are some of the reasons that some churches and denominations reject prophets and prophetic ministry?
3. Have you ever heard a "flaky" prophecy? How did you know it was not a message from the Lord?

4. What are some of the functions of the prophet in the Church?

5. What are some of the ways a person can develop the prophetic anointing?

6. What is the main ingredient in releasing the prophetic anointing?

7. List some dead places where you need to prophesy. Will you step out in faith and do it?

Chapter Five

Apostolic Anointing

Miriam Hellman is a woman who possesses unusual courage. She finds herself in uncommon places doing out-of-the-ordinary things. Life for her is never dull or boring. She has chosen to allow the Lord to send her as His ambassador to do His will on the earth.

AMBASSADORS WITH THE FATHER'S HEART

Recently, Miriam found herself in one of those remarkable places. It all started when she received a prophetic word: "You are a bee. God says you are a bee. The work of the bee is before you. You shall pollinate here and there. A great work of crop pollination shall take place, because you are going to cross-pollinate."

Miriam is an apostolic and prophetic leader. As a woman who reads her Bible regularly, she recognizes the symbolism in a prophetic word. Deborah, whose name meant "bee," was a famous judge in the Bible. Deborah was sent to a man named Barak, and she gave him a prophetic word for the nation. When

Barak received the word, he decided to obey the will and plan of God for his day.

Twenty-four hours after receiving the word about the work of the bee, Miriam heard the Lord speak a prophetic word to her concerning a nation with no hope and no vision. When Miriam received this word, little did she know that God would send her as a Deborah to fulfill His mission to that nation. She did not know that the Lord would soon reveal to her His strategy and destiny for an entire nation.

This prophetic word was taped and transcribed. Later, Miriam's husband sent the transcribed word to three influential businessmen in New York City. Independently, each asked Miriam to go to his homeland, a troubled country across the ocean. They realized she had the ability to raise the hope of their nation.

Because of the volatile political climate of the country, Miriam was in awe, unsure of how to accomplish the mission. So she prayed for the Lord's direction. *Go!* she heard the Lord speak to her spirit, and the Lord gave her the time when she was to go. The businessmen made appointments for Miriam and her husband to meet with government leaders in every settlement of the nation. The two were invited to speak with those in the highest positions of national government.

Miriam's message to the leaders throughout the nation was this: "You need a miracle. You don't have a vision. Without a vision, your people will perish. You don't know who you are or what you are about" (see Prov. 29:18). She told the leaders that Jesus is God's solution.

In one meeting, a key leader urged Miriam, "If you will come here and be with us, we will be with you." This statement is the same invitation that Barak gave to Deborah (see Judg. 4:8). The Lord had sent her as an ambassador with a message from King Jesus, so Miriam accepted the invitation to return with the plan of God and execute a deadly bee sting to the enemy of that nation.

We may never be sent on a mission to speak to the leaders of a foreign government. However, the Lord may send us to deliver a message of hope to someone in the grocery store, the neighborhood or the workplace. Presently, many have no vision for their lives. Because they have no vision, they have no hope. When we are obedient to be sent on small missions, we may later be sent on larger missions. Miriam started out as a housewife who simply responded in obedience to God. She now is being sent by the Lord on strategic missions to the nations of the world. The Lord has an apostolic people who have an ambassadorial assignment. Through the delivery of their messages, a deadly sting is being released to the enemy.

What is an ambassador? Webster defines "ambassador" as "the highest-ranking diplomatic representative appointed by one country or government to represent it in another; an official agent with a special mission; an unofficial representative or messenger."[1]

Apostles and apostolic people are like ambassadors. They are representatives of King Jesus who have been sent throughout the earth to represent the King and His kingdom. Many of these ambassadors do not have official titles, but as informal representatives, they have been sent on special missions by the Lord.

Jesus is the great Apostle of the Church:

Therefore, holy brethren, partakers of a heavenly calling, consider Jesus, the Apostle and High Priest of our confession (Heb. 3:1).

Jesus declared that He was sent by the Father and that He sends an apostolic people to represent Him and fulfill His will on the earth:

As the Father has sent Me, I also send you (John 20:21).

The word "sent" is from the Greek word *apostello*, which means "to send out on a mission; to send away; send forth; to set at liberty."[2] Jesus is an Apostle sent by the Father to set at liberty those who are bound by the enemy (see Luke 4:18).

Apostles are part of the government of the Church. Many times they lead churches or ministries. However, they can be found in every arena of life. These gifts of Jesus are sent on a clear mission from the Lord, and they function as authority figures (see Eph. 4:11,12). Apostles and prophets serve together to lay the foundation for the Church. Jesus, as the Cornerstone, provides the alignment and positioning so the Church can become the glorious temple of the Holy Spirit (see Eph. 2:19-21).

Apostles are visionaries, willing to take risks and to be pioneers. They break open new territories and are powerful spiritual warriors. Apostles are willing to take people into uncharted waters. They have a prophetic vision for the future plans and purposes of God, and they are willing to step out of their comfort zone to follow God. As leaders, they move the Church forward to influence and impact society in a powerful way.

Believers can receive an apostolic anointing. This anointing means they are sent forth by the King into the world to release captives who have been blinded and oppressed by the enemy. Apostolic people have an ambassadorial mission. God will use them to break curses and bring healing to families, cities and nations.

ANOINTED TO HEAL RELATIONSHIPS

The heart of apostolic ministry is the heart of fatherhood. A major mission of apostles and apostolic people is to break the curse of fatherlessness. The last two verses of the Old Testament promise the breaking of this curse:

> Behold, I am going to send you Elijah the prophet before the coming of the great and terrible day of the LORD. And he will restore the hearts of the fathers to their children and the hearts of the children to their fathers, lest I come and smite the land with a curse (Mal. 4:5,6).

Our nation and many nations of the world are afflicted with the curse of fatherlessness. Many fathers are absent from their families, either physically or emotionally. Even the Church has experienced the lack of fathers—spiritual fathers. We have had great theologians, powerful men of God, great teachers and leaders of crusades. Unfortunately, many fathers in the Church have not been willing to pour their lives into spiritual children.

The apostle Paul wrote:

> For if you were to have countless tutors in Christ, yet you would not have many fathers; for in Christ Jesus I became your father through the gospel (1 Cor. 4:15).

Paul was an apostle. He told the Corinthians that he was a father to them. He was not sent just to ensure that their doctrines were correct. He didn't come just to straighten out the problems of the church. He wasn't looking for a place to preach. His ambassadorial assignment was to release the heart of the Father to the Corinthians.

The two letters from Paul to the church at Corinth reveal our great need for spiritual fathers. Many among the Corinthians were coming out of pagan practices. Sin was rampant. The Church was out of order. How they needed a father to help set them free!

Mark Hanby, in his book *You Have Not Many Fathers*, writes about this problem of fatherlessness in the Church:

> One of the results of a fatherless church is oppression (see Isa. 3:5). A family without a father suffers financially, socially and psychologically, as well as spiritually. The pressure on single mothers and fatherless children is oppressive. When a father is not present in a home to train the children in matters of the Lord, the hearts of the children turn to rage and they dishonor authority (see Eph. 6:1-4). Oppression occurs when immature rulers serve as baby-sitters over congregations, leading the people without having any true vision. "Where there is no vision, the people perish" (Prov. 29:18).[3]

John and Paula Sanford are experienced in ministering to those who have suffered from the effects of fatherlessness. Quite early the Sanfords came to the realization that unless hearts of the fathers were turned to their children and the hearts of the children turned to their fathers, it really didn't matter what else was taught or what was accomplished in the churches. The Sanfords are of the opinion that unless there is restoration in this area, an actual curse comes on a people.

The Sanfords have written about Carl Foss, who has a ministry to men in prison. Foss has gathered some alarming statistics concerning young people in prison. He states that between 90 to 95 percent of people in prison have never known the love of a father. The Sanfords describe the sad condition of the hearts of men in a prison where Foss ministers:

> In a visit to a reformatory, speaking to more than forty young people, [Foss] discovered that not one could claim the love of a father. Offering to sit in private with whom-

ever would come to be with a father for fifteen minutes, he was overwhelmed with the response, and with the tears of supposedly hardened tough juveniles. He reported that on McNeil Island, in that prison, a man who had become a prison lawyer, an extremely intelligent man and a competent artist, had prepared a handsome, hand-done Father's Day card, which he offered for sale to his fellow inmates for $4.00. Finding no takers, he reduced the offer to $2.00. Finally, he tried giving the card away. Not one would take a Father's Day card! Stunned, he came to Carl, who said, "Have you spent twenty years in this prison, and you still don't know that not one of these 1280 prisoners has a father who loves him?"[4]

Apostolic people function with the heart of the Father. Therefore, before bringing healing and restoration to others, healing is sometimes needed in their own lives, particularly if they have problems with authority figures. Often it is even difficult to relate to a good and loving Father God if we have not experienced the love and acceptance of a physical father. We may need the heavenly Father's healing before healing others.

How does a person receive healing from fatherlessness? Several steps are helpful:

1. Ask the Lord to reveal any areas of resentment or hurt stemming from your relationship (or lack of one) with your natural father. Sometimes we have ignored the pain and buried it within. When the situation is right, the old hurt surfaces and we say or do things we later regret. The fruit is bad, because there is a bad root.

2. Pray for the Lord to let you see your father (physical or spiritual) through the eyes of the Lord. Since God is an all-knowing and all-seeing God, He knows the rea-

sons for your father's behavior. The reasons may not be godly. We never call evil "good." Only God knows where your father walked in life and what happened to him along the way. We are able to see only what happened to us. Through the eyes of the Lord, we can see truth, not just our hurt. As Jesus hung on the cross, He was able, through the Father's eyes, to see beyond the pain: "Father, forgive them; for they do not know what they are doing" (Luke 23:34).

3. Forgive your father or father figure. Unforgiveness acts like a cancer that will not only destroy you but will also affect those around you: "See to it that no one comes short of the grace of God; that no root of bitterness springing up causes trouble, and by it many be defiled" (Heb. 12:15). A root of bitterness is costly. We cannot afford to allow one to grow in our lives. It can keep us from achieving God's purposes, and it will keep us from bringing positive change into the lives of others.

4. Receive the Father's love. Spend time in His presence. As you talk with Him, listen for Him to speak to you. His voice is the highest voice in the universe. His words will wash away all the negative, hurtful words that have been spoken to you. He wants to affirm His love for you. Wholeness comes only in His presence. Let Him tell you who you *really* are, not who you thought you were or who others said you were.

RECEIVING A NEW IDENTITY

Apostolic people receive a new identity from the Lord. Frequently, people grow up being told that they were a mistake, that they are a failure, that they will never amount to anything in life, that they are stupid and many other hurtful labels. Such people begin to identify with these labels. Before being sent to bring change into the world, they need a change of identity.

Joshua was trained under Moses. He had been a great warrior, but the time came when Joshua was sent as an ambassador to lead the people forth and establish God's will in the Promised Land. However, he could not advance with an old identity. A new name was essential.

Moses understood this principle. He changed Joshua's name from Hoshea to Joshua:

> These are the names of the men whom Moses sent to spy out the land; but Moses called Hoshea [meaning "salvation"] the son of Nun, Joshua [meaning "the Lord saves"] (Num. 13:16).

Moses had been a spiritual father to Joshua, but Joshua would soon take his place as an apostolic leader. The time was coming for Joshua to enter into the purpose for which he was created. His old identity would keep him in an old place, depending on his own strength and abilities. He needed a new name, one that would remind him of his total and complete dependence upon God.

I once read, "A man is not a man until his father tells him he is a man." Joshua needed his spiritual father, Moses, to tell him he was a man—and not just any man, but a man of God.

When Jesus was baptized in the River Jordan, His heavenly Father identified Him as His Son and approved of Him:

> After being baptized, Jesus went up immediately from the water; and behold, the heavens were opened, and he saw the Spirit of God descending as a dove and coming upon Him, and behold, a voice out of the heavens, saying,

"This is My beloved Son, in whom I am well-pleased"
(Matt. 3:16,17).

The Lord gives apostolic people new names and new identities to set them on paths to success.

The nations will see your righteousness, and all kings
your glory; and you will be called by a new name which
the mouth of the LORD will designate (Isa. 62:2).

I minister in Malaysia each year. The country is a Muslim
nation. When the people of Malaysia become Christians, many
change their names. Usually they adopt biblical names like
Joshua, Aaron, Deborah, Rebecca, Paul or Elijah. The new name
gives them a new identity—they are released from their old lives
and recognized as men and women in pursuit of God's purposes.

We greatly need apostolic people who have received a fresh
identity from the Lord. Apostles and apostolic people are desperately needed to restore relationships, both in the family and
in the Church. Ours is a God of restoration. He is raising up
those with an apostolic anointing and sending them on a mission to break the curse of fatherlessness in the land.

APOSTOLIC CHARACTERISTICS

I discuss other characteristics of people with an apostolic
anointing in *A People of Destiny*.[5] Among the characteristics of
apostolic people is that they have spiritual ears to hear what God
is saying and doing:

Now Elijah said to Ahab, "Go up, eat and drink; for there
is the sound of the roar of a heavy shower" (1 Kings 18:41).

Elijah was a prophet with an apostolic anointing. When he was taken to heaven, Elisha, his spiritual son, cried out, "My father, my father" (2 Kings 2:12). Elijah had spiritual ears to hear the sound of coming rain during a time of drought. God gives apostolic people prophetic ears to hear what He has planned for the future.

Furthermore, apostolic people have prophetic eyes. My friend Jean Hodges is anointed to see by the Spirit of God. She was with her husband, Jim, on a ministry trip to Mexico City in 1999. After arriving in the city, she had a vision in which she saw several tectonic plates that looked as if they were in the ground underneath Mexico City. Then she saw the plates suddenly shift.

Jean shared what she had seen with several others who were with her. The next day, while her group was worshiping the Lord during a church service, the building started shaking. When they heard the news reports later, Jean's vision was confirmed. Tectonic plates beneath the surface of the earth had shifted. Jean had prophetic eyes to see an earthquake before it happened. Apostolic people see things by the Spirit of God before they are evident to physical eyes.

Apostolic people also allow the Lord to position them to be used by Him. In the Bible we read the story of Ruth, who had an apostolic anointing. She was "a sent one." Ruth was sent to fulfill God's purposes for her life. She could have remained in the familiar land of Moab. After all, she understood the culture, and her family and old relationships were in Moab. Ruth made a courageous decision to leave the comfortable and familiar. She would go where God was moving.

Naomi, Ruth's mother-in-law, urged her daughters-in-law, Ruth and Orpah, to depart from her and go to their own families. Both had to consider the cost. Similarly, in making a decision to follow the Lord, believers must count the cost. Friends and family will not always agree with this decision. Rejection and persecution are sometimes the result of obedience to the Lord.

Orpah kissed Naomi and returned to the old place. She was easily persuaded to go back to the comfortable and familiar. But Ruth clung to Naomi. She made a firm declaration never to return to the old, lifeless place again. The destiny of the Lord for Ruth was tied to the new place. A repositioning was necessary for the Lord's purposes.

You and I today are the recipients of Ruth's obedience. In the new place she met Boaz. They became the parents of Obed, who was the father of Jesse and the grandfather of King David. From David's lineage came Jesus, our Lord and Savior. One small step of obedience can lead to great things in the kingdom of God!

Apostolic anointing will grace us for the work God has purposed for our lives.

The positioning of the believer to fulfill God's purposes may be a place of employment. It may be a neighborhood. The Lord is positioning apostolic people in every arena of life to extend His kingdom. An apostolic anointing will grace us for the position God has purposed for our lives. It may not be a comfortable place; it may not be familiar. The important thing is that we allow Him to put us where His purposes can be accomplished through us.

Apostolic people have an anointing of power from the Holy Spirit. Spiritual equipment is given to do the work God has called them to do. The Spirit empowers them to do what they cannot normally do. An apostolic anointing, flowing from the heart of the Father, gives forth a sweet aroma in the earth.

One of the ingredients in the anointing oil of the Old Testament had a pleasant aroma. Cinnamon has a sweet odor and is used for flavoring. The fragrance of the cinnamon served to counteract the stench of the sacrifices in the Tabernacle. Since everything in the Tabernacle was anointed, what a sweet-smelling place it must have been!

Have you ever walked into a mall that had one of those wonderful cinnamon-roll shops? Maybe you and your friend just finished a big lunch, and you decided to do a little shopping. As soon as you walked into the mall, you smelled the sweet aroma of the cinnamon rolls. You and your friend agreed that you didn't need one of those delicious pastries after such a big lunch. However, the longer you smelled the cinnamon, the more you weakened to the temptation. Soon the two of you were heading directly for the cinnamon-roll shop. But you decided you would buy only one roll and split it between the two of you. Arriving at the shop, you discovered that other people had been drawn by the same fragrance. There was a line, and you had to wait your turn to place your order. The longer you stood in line, the better it smelled. Finally, you and your friend *each* ordered a roll—just this once, of course. After eating an entire roll, you said to each other, "I can't believe I ate the whole thing!"

The apostolic anointing is like the cinnamon. Upon those with apostolic gifts a sweet fragrance is released that counteracts the stench of a hopeless, sinful world. The Father's heart flows forth to set free the oppressed and break the curse of fatherlessness. We may not all be apostles, but we all can receive an apostolic anointing. May the Lord anoint us with sweet cinnamon and send us as His ambassadors to extend His kingdom into every arena of life!

DISCUSSION QUESTIONS

1. Describe some of the functions of an ambassador. How is an ambassador similar to an apostle or apostolic people?
2. What are some of the results of fatherlessness? In the home? In the Church?
3. How can a person be healed from the pain of fatherlessness?
4. What is one of your old names? What is the new name the Lord has given you? Ask Him to speak your new identity to you.
5. Where have you been positioned to release an apostolic anointing? Ask the Lord to give you a fresh empowering for your task.
6. Describe a person you now recognize as having an apostolic anointing.
7. How is cinnamon similar to the apostolic anointing?
8. Are you giving forth a sweet smell to those around you?

Chapter Six

Anointing for Intercession

"We have a powerful intercessor in our church," the pastor excitedly reported upon my arrival at the airport. "Whenever I need prayer for anything, he is the one I go to. This intercessor will keep praying until there is a breakthrough."

"Every pastor needs an intercessor like that," I responded. As the discussion continued, it centered on the need for strong intercession in the local church. We talked about the awareness of a greater need for prayer and pray-ers if we are going to see the Lord's victory in lives and cities throughout the earth.

ANSWERING GOD'S CALL

During my ministry at the church, a man named Mark came to me and shared some of his testimony. "While you were here last year, you spoke a prophetic word to me. Part of the word was that I am called to be an intercessor. You said God would begin to give me an understanding of the things the Lord wanted me to pray.

"At that time I had never thought about being an intercessor. I didn't really know much about intercession and certainly had never seen myself doing that," Mark explained enthusiastically. "After you prophesied over me, you laid hands on me and asked the Lord to impart an anointing for intercession to me. Something dramatic happened! I started *wanting* to intercede. There were times when I would wake up during the night and find myself praying. I started praying about things I had no previous knowledge of. Later, I would discover that the Lord had answered my prayers. Now, all I want to do is to intercede. I don't care if I ever do anything else, as long as I can pray and intercede."

After the service, the pastor mentioned that he saw me talking with Mark. "That's the man who is my most faithful intercessor," the pastor responded. "He is the one I was telling you about when you arrived at the airport."

How wonderful! The Lord had taken Mark, an ordinary believer, and turned him into the most powerful intercessor in the congregation. Rather than being just an idle person sitting in church, he was now active in the Lord's work. Mark is not part of an elite group of Christians. He is not one of God's favorites. He is merely a believer who is faithfully doing what God has called him to do.

THE IMPORTANCE OF INTERCESSION

What do I mean by intercession? According to the dictionary, to "intercede" means "to plead or make a request in behalf of another or others [to 'intercede' with the authorities for the prisoner]; to intervene for the purpose of producing agreement; mediate."[1]

In intercession we are pleading with our heavenly Authority for the release of prisoners bound by the enemy. Prisoners are those bound by sin, false religions, sickness, disease or attacks of Satan. These people need someone to stand between them and the enemy. They need someone to lay one hand on them and one on God.

This need for an intercessor was expressed through Job:

> For [God] is not a man as I am that I may answer Him, that we may go to court together. There is no umpire between us, who may lay his hand upon us both (Job 9:32,33).

Job was crying out for someone to mediate his case in the heavenly courtroom. He needed an arbitrator to argue his case with the righteous Judge. Jesus was the answer to Job's cry. Today, intercessors, as Jesus' representatives on the earth, are used by the Lord to mediate between man and God.

The Hebrew word for intercession is *paga*. Some of the meanings of the word "intercession," according to *Strong's Concordance*, are "to come between, cause to entreat, fall upon, make intercession, light upon, meet together, pray, reach, run."[2]

Discussing intercession as a meeting, Dutch Sheets writes:

> A meeting can be a good and pleasant experience, or it can be a violent confrontation between opposing forces. The intercessor is either going to *meet* with God for the purpose of reconciling the world to the Father and His wonderful blessings, or he is going to *meet* satanic forces of opposition to enforce the victory of Calvary. The purpose will vary, but one thing is certain: The prayers of an understanding intercessor WILL create a *meeting*. And when the *meeting* comes to a close, something will have changed.[3]

Vijeyrani is an intercessor who lives in Sri Lanka. She lives below a *kovil*, a Hindu temple. Services are held and sacrifices are made in the kovil. The people in this area have little hope for the future. These indigenous people are of a socioeconomic status that uses public wells for bathing. Vijeyrani and another Christian, Miriam, live on the same street. This street, named Mosque Lane for a nearby mosque, is also home to Buddhists, Hindus and Muslims. Christians have been walking, praying and meeting in a cell group under the guidance of Miriam, who is in leadership at Emmanuel Church. Several people have recently come to Vijeyrani's home and received Jesus as their Lord and Savior.

One lady cannot go to church because of persecution in the family. She meets with Vijeyrani for one hour every day to pray. One day a friend, who did not know about the prayer meeting, stopped by unexpectedly, so she joined them in prayer. The power of God was so strong, she fell to the floor and cried out to God because of the bitterness and unforgiveness in her heart. These ladies had never seen anything like it. However, the friend knew it was the power of God. This meeting lasted three hours!

All this and more is happening in a believer's home below a Hindu kovil. These believers stand between lost people and the enemy for the purpose of reconciling these people to the Lord. Because of this intercession, lives are being forever changed, as many are receiving Jesus into their hearts. These prayer warriors are confident that intercession will change their city and their nation.

A COVENANT RELATIONSHIP

God has always chosen to do His work of intercession on Earth through those who have a covenant relationship with Him. I talk about this in my book *Prophetic Intercession*:

Moses was willing to stand in the gap for God's people (see Ps. 106:23). However, Jesus was the only one worthy to pay the price through His death, burial and resurrection, and to stand in the gap and repair the wall separating God and man. Because of what He did, He bought back what man had given away. Jesus then restored humanity's legal authority to be God's representatives on Earth, so God's plan for man would ultimately be fulfilled. Man could once again rule through the Messiah, Jesus. The Lord extends His goodness into all nations, because His people participate with the Lord in redeeming the earth. His representative would be the one Ezekiel said God looked for to stand in the gaps, or breeches. . . .

The Lord is raising up intercessors that will stand in the gaps to intercede. As God's covenant partners, they will become the voice of the Lord in the earth to speak forgiveness, healing and restoration to the broken places needing repair. He is looking for those who are in covenant with Him. That means you and me.[4]

Every believer, to one degree or another, is called to pray and intercede. Some people seem to have a greater call and gifting for intercession; however, all of us should be intercessors. We should desire to communicate with the Lord and partner with Him in His desires for mankind.

I like what my friend Beth Alves says about our responsibility and privilege to pray:

Christians are called to a lifestyle of prayer, but many have come to see prayer as nothing more than calling upon their Heavenly Butler for daily service, or crying out to their Heavenly Lifeguard when they are drowning in their daily circumstances. Certainly God has more for us than that. Jesus said that because he was going to the Father, we would do even greater works than He did (see

John 14:12). When He spoke those words, He was not talking to a crowd of world-renowned Christian evangelists. No, He was speaking to every person who names Jesus as Lord and Savior. He was speaking to you and me.

Prayer is the responsibility of every Christian. God's Word tells us to pray. But we don't pray just because we have to; we pray because talking to God is a privilege. Prayer is entering into relationship with God so we can determine His will in the matter and call His will into existence upon the earth.[5]

Intercession is the most unselfish thing a person can do. It is not praying for one's self; it is praying for others. It is praying for God's will to be done on the earth. Intercessors not only pray for individuals; they also pray for their cities and territories to be transformed. A cry must ascend to God from our cities if He is going to bring transformation to our towns and regions. God is now raising up intercessors who will cry out for revival and transformation to take place in their cities.

Abraham interceded for the city of Sodom (see Gen. 18). The first earnest prayer recorded in the Bible is Abraham's prayer for the city of Sodom to be spared. His heart was filled with compassion as he cried out. Abraham knew the Judge of all the earth would do the right thing. He did not plead that the wicked would be excused and God would overlook their evil deeds. Abraham pleaded for the city to be spared for the sake of God's righteous covenant people living in that place. As a result of Abraham's intercession, Lot and his family were delivered.

Today we can see the potential for the greatest revival in the history of the Church. Many prophets and church leaders are prophesying about coming revival. Intercession is one of the major components that will release this mighty outpouring of the Lord. Frank Damazio seems to agree:

> There has always been a spirit of prayer and intercession associated with spiritual awakening, both in Scripture and in history. Revival is preceded by prayer, birthed through intercession and sustained by fervent, persevering prayer. Prayer is the central living element to every spiritual awakening and every moving of the Holy Spirit.[6]

INTERCESSORS NEED ONE ANOTHER

Most intercessors I meet express a need to be connected with other intercessors in a city. There is a realization that they need each other. Several reasons are usually given for the desire to know other intercessors. One of the reasons intercessors want to come together is that there is a discernible increase in spiritual power: "How could one chase a thousand, and two put ten thousand to flight unless . . . the LORD had given them up?" (Deut. 32:30).

In *Prophetic Intercession*, I wrote about the difficulties we were experiencing in the ministry several years ago. Although we had many intercessors around the nation who were praying for us, we did not have corporate intercession. After the Lord revealed to us this area of weakness, we started several intercessory prayer groups that would intercede for us. We saw an immediate change. A vicious cycle of accidents and harassments stopped.

Intercessors strive to hear the Lord correctly. One way of doing this is to listen for affirmation that others are hearing the same spiritual messages. One of the ways we test our spiritual hearing is by listening to other prophetic voices in the Body of Christ. We have found that the Lord often confirms His word to us by speaking it to others we respect. This helps assure us that it is the Lord's voice we are hearing.

When intercessors get together, sharing information helps them target their prayers. I remember taking a physical education course in school. One of the things we learned was how to use a bow and arrow. We worked hard to get our arrows near the bull's-eye. Although it was great just to hit the target, I was not satisfied with that. I wanted the bull's-eye! That's the way intercessors are. They want to be more effective in prayer, and they need information to help them do that.

AM I ANOINTED FOR INTERCESSION?

How, then, can we know we have an anointing for intercession? First, the Lord will let us know. He wants us to know what He has called us to do. We will have a "knowing" on the inside—God's Spirit will cause our spirit to know that He has anointed us for intercession.

Many times insecurities, feelings of inferiority and fears of unworthiness will try to rob us of God's purposes. I remember attending a meeting on prayer many years ago. At the end of the service, the speaker asked for those who were intercessors to come to the front of the room. I knew that I prayed much of the time, and I loved to pray. But was I an intercessor? My mind started rationalizing: *You don't know enough to be a real intercessor. Others are much more powerful in the Spirit than you are. What makes you think God could ever use you that way?* This diatribe persisted as I sat there, listening to the old familiar tapes rerun in my mind. As a result, I never went forward. Later, as I left the meeting, I tried to justify my lack of action to the Lord: "I know there are others far more qualified than I am, Father. There are those who are much more spiritual. But, Lord, if there is any way you can make me one of your intercessors, I volunteer."

I did not realize that the Lord was the one who gave me the desire for intercession, that it did not come from me. As we follow the Lord, He gives us desires that help us find His will for our lives. God does not want us to search and never find His will. He is not that kind of God. In fact, His Word promises that when we delight ourselves in Him, He will give us the desires of our heart (see Ps. 37:4). God will grant those holy desires—in His time—because He is the one who gave them to us.

As I developed a greater desire for intercession, I found others who loved to pray. Getting together to pray became a highlight of my days. When I prayed with others, I seemed to have a greater understanding of the things God wanted me to pray about. Revelation of the heart of God increased.

Another way we can know we have an anointing for intercession is that other people will start to identify us as intercessors. It will not be necessary to announce to others that we have this anointing. If we are faithful to pray and join with other intercessors, before long we will be recognized as intercessors.

When we regularly exercise our intercessory gifting, the anointing increases.

My spiritual muscles increased as I participated in prayer with various intercessors and intercessory groups. Just being around others with an anointing for intercession caused my own anointing to grow. The more I prayed with them, the more the anointing increased. I call this exercising my spiritual muscles.

When a person fails to use a physical muscle, it becomes weak and lifeless. The same thing happens spiritually. When we fail to use our spiritual muscles on a consistent basis, they atrophy. In times of urgency, they are not able to function properly.

But when we exercise our intercessory gifting on a regular basis, the anointing increases. The anointing will then empower us in such a way as to produce miracles.

Seeing the Bigger Picture

We can see a picture of the anointing for intercession in the Old Testament anointing ointment. One ingredient in the ointment was a plant called cassia (see Exod. 30:24). Cassia is a bitter medicine, but one that purges and heals those who use it. The shrub only grows at great heights of 8,000 feet and above.[7]

In Texas, where I live, there are few great heights or mountains. However, I have visited places around the world that have tall, majestic mountains. On some of those mountains, I noticed, trees grow up to a certain elevation. When I asked a local resident why there were no trees higher up on their mountain, I was told that trees are not able to survive above a certain height.

Not so with cassia. Cassia grows on great heights, flourishing where other plants cannot exist. Intercessors are like cassia. They seem to thrive as they reach new heights in the Spirit. There is an intense longing to be blessed with every spiritual blessing in heavenly places with Christ Jesus (see Eph. 1:3). Intercessors respond to the cry of the Lord's heart, as He calls them up out of the ordinary and invites them to a higher place.

> After these things I looked, and behold, a door standing open in heaven, and the first voice which I had heard, like the sound of a trumpet speaking with me, said, "Come up here, and I will show you what must take place after these things" (Rev. 4:1).

The Lord invites intercessors to new heights so He can show them things that are to come. He reveals His desire for people and cities. Intercessors are not limited to information from newspapers, TV or the Internet. They are not limited to what their eyes see or ears hear. The Lord gives them information supernaturally so they can be more effective in praying for breakthrough.

I once read a story about two young brothers watching a parade. One brother named Johnny was on the ground, watching the parade from behind a fence, because he was too short to peer over it. His ability to see was limited to the knothole in the fence. Johnny's older brother, James, climbed up on top of the fence to watch the parade.

As the parade moved down the street, Johnny watched the marching band as it passed. He saw animals in cages being pulled down the street, followed by girls twirling batons. Then there was nothing. As Johnny continued to look through the small knothole in the fence, he couldn't see anything happening. "Is the parade over?" he asked, thinking there was nothing more to see. James called down to him, "Come up here, Johnny. You can see much better from here."

After climbing up onto the fence, Johnny had a different perspective on the parade. The parade was not limited to a few participants, and it was not over. He had just been in a lower place, where his visibility was restricted. In the higher place, he could see the entire parade, from beginning to end.

The Lord is like that. He sees the entire parade of life, from beginning to end. Our vision can be limited by earthly circumstances, and we may think the parade is over. We tend to believe nothing is happening. If we will respond to the call of the Spirit to "come up higher," the Lord will show us those things that must shortly take place. We can then participate with the Lord by interceding for His will to be done on Earth. An anointing for intercession from this place will release God's transforming power for individuals, cities and the nations of the world.

DISCUSSION QUESTIONS

1. Give a simple definition of intercession.
2. Why is intercession necessary? Can't God just do what He wants to do?
3. Discuss the importance of intercession in city transformation. Why do intercessors in a city have a need to know each other?
4. How can the anointing for intercession be increased?
5. How is the plant cassia a picture of intercessors?
6. Whom does the Lord call to be intercessors? How do you know whether or not you are an intercessor?
7. Have you ever heard old tapes in your mind talking to you about intercession? What did they say? What did you do?
8. Have you interceded for someone today?

Chapter Seven

Corporate Anointing

Fall is my favorite season of the year. Maybe it is because the cooler weather is so refreshing after the long, hot summers in Texas. It could be the change of the colors, as the leaves on trees turn to bright gold and deep red. Fall reminds me of the warmth of logs burning in the fireplace and the wonderful fragrance of candles glowing in the dark. These are only a few reasons that autumn holds such a fond place in my heart.

THE NEED FOR A TEAM MENTALITY

When I think of fall, I remember watching flocks of geese as they flew overhead to their winter home. Watching them is fascinating as they soar together. Through the years I often wondered about these small creatures.

How are they able to fly in such a perfect V formation? How do they have the strength to fly such long distances? What happens if one of the birds gets sick or wounded?

Many times the Lord helps us see a picture of His will for us through animals or nature. The geese flying in formation are a

visible representation of the way the Body of Christ is to function.

When geese are flying in *V* formation, each bird flaps its
wings. The flapping of the wings of a bird will cause uplift for
the bird following. Each bird, as a result of the other birds'
efforts, receives greater strength for the journey. If one bird falls
out of formation, it experiences greater drag and resistance as it
tries to fly alone. The amount of strength and energy needed to
perform the task of flying is greatly increased.

At times the goose flying the point position gets tired. He
rotates back in the formation, and another goose takes his place
and flies point. One goose is not required to carry the full responsibility for the entire trip.

If a goose gets sick or is wounded by gunshot, it falls out of
formation. Two other geese also fall out to lend help or protection until the wounded bird has recovered. The corporate mind-
set seems to motivate these geese in all they do. In fact, some of
the geese flying toward the back of the formation will honk to
encourage those up front!

We need this type of corporate mind-set in the Body of Christ.
Most people, particularly in our Western culture, do not have a
corporate mind-set. Instead, they have an individual viewpoint.
God does not want us to lose our uniqueness, but He does want
us to discover the power of togetherness.

Heaven is a picture of God's togetherness and His will for
the earth. That is why Jesus taught His disciples to pray that the
will of God being done in heaven would come to the earth: "Thy
kingdom come. Thy will be done, on earth as it is in heaven"
(Matt. 6:10). The corporate anointing began in heaven. The
Godhead—Father, Son and Holy Spirit—work together. Angels
are in total unity with heaven's will.

Lucifer tried to sow discord in heaven. He had an individual
viewpoint and not a corporate mind-set:

But you said in your heart, "I will ascend to heaven; I will raise my throne above the stars of God, and I will sit on the mount of assembly in the recesses of the north. I will ascend above the heights of the clouds; I will make myself like the Most High" (Isa. 14:13,14).

Lucifer led a rebellion in heaven among the angels, and he and the angels who followed him were cast out of heaven. Discord and rebellion can have no part of heaven; neither are they part of God's will for the earth.

DISCORD AND DISUNITY SOWED IN THE GARDEN

God created man and woman to walk together as His representatives on the earth. They were to portray on Earth a picture of what heaven is like. However, Satan did not stop with his intent to destroy the corporate plan of God, even after being cast out of heaven. He came to the garden to cause conflict between heaven and Earth. He sowed rebellion, deception and disunity in the man and the woman, Adam and Eve (see Gen. 3). The man and woman listened to the enemy, and sin deharmonized everything!

Thousands of years later, Jesus, through His death, burial and resurrection, made the way for heaven and Earth to be brought back into harmony. The Church became God's agent for the ongoing reconciliation of heaven and Earth. God would use a people with a corporate anointing to do that which none of us individually could ever do. Earth still has the potential of looking like heaven.

A corporate mind-set can be seen in the Early Church. The Bible records how believers frequently gathered together. They

devoted themselves to God and to each other. They were stead-
fast and faithful to see God's will come to the earth:

> They were continually devoting themselves to the apos-
> tles' teaching and to fellowship, to the breaking of
> bread and to prayer. . . . Day by day continuing with one
> mind in the temple, and breaking bread from house to
> house, they were taking their meals together with glad-
> ness and sincerity of heart, praising God and having
> favor with all the people. And the Lord was adding to
> their number day by day those who were being saved
> (Acts 2:42,46,47).

The corporate anointing released multiplication and a harvest
of souls.

REESTABLISHING TRUST AND UNITY

The team concept is vital to a corporate anointing. Corporate
teams are established through relationships and the ability to
trust. Many people have difficulty trusting. They have been
involved in relationships in which trust has been broken, possibly with friends, family, children or a spouse. Broken relationships also can occur in business or ministry. Hurt people find it
difficult to trust or to know who can be trusted. Once trust is
broken, it can be very difficult to restore.

Questions asked by many when trust has been broken include:

- How do I begin to trust again?
- Whom do I trust?
- How do I develop trust?

• How far should I go in trusting?

• How do I know I will not get hurt by trusting again?

As believers, we often think we are supposed to trust everyone. That is simply not true. Trust is developed as we see that a person is trustworthy. Jesus knew that not all people could be trusted. He warned His disciples to be careful in their relationships:

> Do not give what is holy to dogs, and do not throw your pearls before swine, lest they trample them under their feet, and turn and tear you to pieces (Matt. 7:6).

Jesus Himself discerned whom He would trust:

> But Jesus, on His part, was not entrusting Himself to them, for He knew all men, and because He did not need anyone to testify concerning man, for He Himself knew what was in man (John 2:24,25).

Jesus knew human beings were untrustworthy; therefore, He did not commit Himself to everyone.

Paul instructed his spiritual son Timothy to carefully commit himself to those he could trust before pouring his life into them:

> The things which you have heard from me in the presence of many witnesses, these entrust to faithful men, who will be able to teach others also (2 Tim. 2:2).

There is a difference between love and trust. We are called to love all people with the love of the Lord. However, we are not called to trust all people. Trust must be earned.

By the time my children reached the age of 12, they wanted to drive the family car. I can remember their reasons:

- "I am sure I can drive the car. I have been watching you and Dad drive for years."
- "Just let me drive around the block. You will see that I can drive."
- "All the other kids are driving their parents' cars."

How they wanted to be able to drive the car! In my children's minds they could find no reason why they should not be trusted to do so. I told them, "I love you very much. But I do not trust you for one minute behind the wheel." The reason I did not trust them was they had no training or experience. They had done nothing to earn trust in driving. However, none of that changed my love for them. We are to love people with the love of God, but we do not have to trust them when trust has not been earned.

Love is not just a feeling. We are to love others with God's unconditional love, not our limited human love. We must learn to separate people from their actions so we can love them, even if we do not approve of their behavior or choices. We may need to ask the Lord to allow us to see a person through His eyes and not our own.

I remember a college English professor I had many years ago. She had a way of insulting and intimidating the students, even though there were some really great kids in the class. The professor would call the students up to the front of the class and make them feel as if they were stupid, miserable failures. After several months in her class, I found myself resenting her. I didn't like anything about her. I didn't trust her, and I didn't want to be around her. Then the Lord started dealing with me.

"Barbara, you see *what* she does; I see *why* she does it," the Lord told me. I started asking Him to let me see the *why*, and I soon became aware of little things. She had a problem with one of her knees, causing her to be up all night with pain. When she came to class, she was tired and hurting. She often spoke of painful relationships in her personal life. I was seeing things about her I had not noticed before. All I had seen in the past was her bad behavior.

After noticing some of these things, I asked the Lord to help me to make her a "love project." I would *will* myself to love her until I could actually feel it. It took some time, but as I forgave her and made the decision to love her, the Lord did the work in my heart. I did not love or excuse her wrong behavior, but I loved *her* with God's love. She did not know the Lord; without Him in her life, she was a helpless, miserable person. She eventually visited with me, and I was able to encourage her. I asked the Lord to continue to send laborers into her path after I finished the class. Sometimes it helps to make love projects of difficult people in our lives.

Several other steps are advantageous in learning to trust again. First of all, we must ask the Lord to help us forgive the person who violated our trust. Forgiveness does not mean we can immediately trust the person again; it does mean that God can open the door for healing to begin. We forgive when we don't know what the other person will do. All expectations from the other person must be released. Sometimes we think if we forgive, the other person will respond in a certain way. Those expectations of positive response have to be dropped. We must forgive because it is the Lord's will. We forgive, whether or not the other person responds by doing the right thing.

The next step in learning to trust is to forgive ourselves. Remember, we are in a process of growth. We are not perfect. It is important to remember that we are not failures but are simply in a period of learning. I sometimes call this the School of the Spirit. These lessons can be difficult, but they are invaluable for life and for the future.

Finally, we must forgive God. This may sound silly, as He has not done anything wrong, but we sometimes think He has. We may have prayed and not seen the answer we had hoped for. Remember, there can be another person's will involved in the situation. God will not change anyone's will. He gives each of us

God is lifting up a corporate people who will help advance His Kingdom.

a choice, and people don't always choose God's will—or ours either, for that matter! When we find ourselves upset with God for seemingly not answering our prayers, we need to ask Him to forgive us for our wrong attitude toward Him.

CORPORATE ANOINTING FOR VICTORY

God is lifting up a corporate people who will help advance His Kingdom. These people will encounter warfare. One of the ingredients of the anointing ointment was a plant called sweet calamus. Calamus is a sweet cane, or reed, that grows in miry soil, but it stands upright. The more the bark of the plant is beaten, the sweeter it becomes.

Sweet calamus is a picture of the anointing needed in warfare. The more we are attacked and persecuted, the more sweet calamus we need in our lives. Warfare can make us bitter, or it can make us better. We have a choice. Remember, the Bible warns us not to let bitterness get into our hearts (see Heb. 12:15).

A root of bitterness will not only pollute us, but it will also cor-
rupt many.

Years ago, a man pastored a church. Life went well for a period of time. Then problems began to surface between the pastor
and the congregation. The pastor lashed out at the congregation
from the pulpit. The congregation, in turn, started lashing out
at the pastor. Soon there was war in the church. Before long, the
congregation asked the pastor to resign. Reluctantly, he did so.

Hurt and wounded, he wandered around for a while, trying
to decide what to do. *Do I want to serve God? Should I be in the ministry? Maybe I should not be involved with church and with Christians.*
Finally, he decided to start another church. However, a root of
bitterness had formed in his heart. Bitterness can usually be
detected in a person's speech, and this man's words were filled
with hurt and bitterness that he had not dealt with.

Young people with their own roots of bitterness started following the former pastor. Spirits attract like spirits; familiar
spirits will find each other. The root of bitterness had now
turned to deception. The former pastor and his followers rejected society, marking it off as doomed simply because it did not
see things as they did. The leader claimed he was the prophet of
the hour, with God's word in his mouth.

Occultism soon entered the group, and immorality quickly
followed. I was in Canada several years ago and watched a video
produced by this organization. They had an evangelistic tool
called Flirty Fishing. Their young people would go out on the
streets and seduce other young men and women. They would
take them home and sleep with them to show them "the love of
God." As a result, the group grew tremendously—a root of bitterness defiling many!

The price of bitterness is high. When we realize a root of bitterness is trying to take hold of our lives, we must do whatever is
necessary to get rid of it. Prayer is the key—sweet communion

with God. We must stay on our knees until the work is complete and we are healed. In the midst of warfare, we can allow the sweet calamus of God's love to cause us to become better, not bitter.

The corporate anointing flows through those who have tasted the sweetness of victory in warfare. They have dealt with issues of trust and are learning to trust once again. A realization has come that as God puts teams of people together, a greater power is released. In fact, this is a principle known in physics as synergy.

Synergy is a "combined or cooperative action or force."[1] Synergy occurs when there is a simultaneous action of separate agencies working together. The total effect of the effort is greater than the sum of the individual efforts. There is a similar principle in the Bible that says one can chase a thousand, but two working together can chase 10,000 (see Deut. 32:30). The enemy is aware of this principle, which is why he is always trying to divide God's people. If he can separate us and keep us from walking in unity, he can strip us of the exponential power God has made available.

Kelly Varner addresses this topic in his book *Corporate Anointing*:

> The purpose of every enemy of Israel in the Old Testament was to *keep the Israelites from becoming a nation*, a people unto God. The devil, the ultimate enemy of mankind and of God's purposes for us, made every attempt to *abort the Messianic seed* and to destroy or contaminate the Israelites' corporate effectiveness. This same demonic attitude was especially apparent in the actions of the Edomites, who were direct descendants of Esau. . . . The enemy will do everything to frustrate *your* understanding and pursuit of corporate anointing as well—but that doesn't mean you should helplessly stand aside while his efforts succeed.[2]

The Lord's physical body was taken to heaven. Nevertheless, He promised to have a spiritual Body on the earth. It is only as we are joined together that we can manifest the Body of Christ in the world:

> From whom the whole body, being fitted and held together by that which every joint supplies, according to the proper working of each individual part, causes the growth of the body for the building up of itself in love (Eph. 4:16).

The phrase "fitted and held together" is from the Greek word *sunarmologeo*. Sunarmologeo means to join closely together, as in framing the parts of a building—or members of the Body. The word "joint" is from the Greek word *haphe*, meaning a bond or connection.

Paul was saying to the church of Ephesus that God is joining His people together and framing His Body on the earth. Each individual joint or connection is important. Together, the corporate Body of Christ will cause growth. In other words, there will be an increase. Not only will there be spiritual growth in the members of the Body, but also lost people will be saved. Revival will occur, and the blessings of God will be released:

> Behold, how good and how pleasant it is for brothers to dwell together in unity! It is like the precious oil upon the head, coming down upon the beard, even Aaron's beard, coming down upon the edge of his robes. It is like the dew of Hermon, coming down upon the mountains of Zion; for there the LORD commanded the blessing— life forever (Ps. 133:1-3).

Aaron, the high priest mentioned in this psalm, had 12 stones on the breastplate of his garment. The stones represented the 12 tribes of Israel. Each tribe was important. When the oil of anointing was poured over the head of the high priest, it ran down from his head and poured over the stones, representing his receiving of the anointing for the entire nation. This is a picture of the corporate anointing in unity, joining each of us together in the Body of Christ. God then commands blessings upon us. The new wine of revival is poured out, miracles happen, and a new evangelistic power is released for a great harvest of souls.

The ingredient of olive oil in the anointing ointment is a picture of the corporate anointing of the Holy Spirit on a group of people, not just on an individual. All the individual ingredients of the anointing ointment were dry without the oil. When the various ingredients were mixed with the oil, the entire mixture became holy.

A few years ago, at the Seattle Special Olympics, nine contestants, all physically or mentally disabled, assembled at the starting line for the 100-meter dash. At the gun they all started out, not exactly in a dash, but with an inclination to run the race to the finish and win. All, that is, except one little boy who stumbled on the asphalt, tumbled over a couple of times and began to cry.

The other eight heard the boy's cry. They slowed down and looked behind them. Then they all turned around and went back—every one of them. One girl with Down's syndrome bent down and kissed him, saying, "This will make it feel better." Then all nine linked arms and walked together to the finish line.

Everyone in the stadium stood, and the cheering went on for several minutes. People who were there still tell the story. Why? Because deep down we know that what matters in this life is more than winning for ourselves. What matters is helping others win, even if it means slowing down and changing our own course.

Individually, we are the spices of the anointing ointment. Together, there is a corporate anointing that is released when we are blended together. Only then will we see the full ministry and anointing of Jesus on the earth.

DISCUSSION QUESTIONS

1. Discuss the corporate anointing found in heaven.
2. Are there trust issues in your life that need to be healed? What are the steps toward being able to trust again?
3. What is a love project? Is there one you need to work on?
4. Who needs to be forgiven when trust has been broken?
5. What is the meaning of separating the person from the behavior? How do you do this?
6. Describe what happens when a root of bitterness defiles someone.
7. What is synergy? How does the corporate anointing release this dynamic?
8. Are you allowing yourself to become bitter or better?

Chapter Eight

Marketplace Anointing

Thanksgiving is a special time of the year. Since the time of the early settlers in the United States, people have set aside time in the autumn to remember the goodness of God and to thank Him for His provision during the year. For a number of years, my husband has been asked by his company to share the history of Thanksgiving and pray over the food for the annual company dinner.

MISSIONARIES IN THE MARKETPLACE

Dale is an engineer and plant manager for his company. To others it is evident that he is a solid believer in Jesus. Through the years, he has built strong relationships with the supervisors who work with him. Lunchtime usually finds Dale and some of the supervisors eating together in the break room. One of these supervisors is a Vietnamese lady named Hanh Singh.

On one of those days, Dale and Hanh were having lunch together with another worker. Hanh, the legal guardian of her four grandchildren, expressed her distress and anxiety over some problems in her family. Dale took the opportunity to share with Hanh about the love of Jesus. He explained how Jesus died for her and wanted to give her eternal life. "Look!" Hanh exclaimed. "I have goose bumps all over me!" Hanh received a supernatural touch from the Lord, and she recognized immediately the undeniable, manifest power of Jesus.

Several days later, Hanh and her husband rode to church with us. At the end of the service that Sunday morning, Dale had the privilege of praying with Hanh, as she invited Jesus to be her Savior.

A few weeks after this, Dale helped set up a meeting for Hanh and several members of her family with a Vietnamese pastor. They were able to hear, in their own language, the message of Jesus' offer of salvation.

The next day one of Hanh's coworkers returned to her job after being absent due to a car accident. She expressed her concern over a physical problem, and Hanh told her that Jesus could heal her. She then held the lady's hands and prayed. The following day the lady excitedly told Hanh the physical problem had disappeared.

Soon another worker came to Hanh. She had gone through surgery a few weeks before, and now her stomach was swollen and painful to the touch. The doctor was contemplating another surgery to correct the condition. Hanh asked the lady if she could pray for her. "All you have to do is believe," she told her. "The Lord will heal you." The woman agreed, and Hanh prayed for her. Within 24 hours the lady's stomach became soft and returned to its normal size. When the lady went back to her doctor, she was able to tell him how she had been healed by God's power.

Today, Hanh is being used by the Lord as a missionary in the marketplace. She prays with workers who are in distress, those who are angry and upset and those who need the healing power of Jesus. In fact, some of the people in the plant lovingly call her "Doctor." Of course, she always lets them know she is not a doctor, and she then tells them about the Great Physician, Jesus Christ, who can heal their bodies, bring peace to their minds and give them eternal life.

Whenever Hanh is unsure what to say or do, she asks Dale. He has been able to help her grow in her walk with the Lord. As a result, the Lord is using her in a powerful way in her place of employment. Dale and Hanh both have a marketplace anointing.

NOT CONFINED TO A BUILDING

The anointing is not confined to a church building or Christian gatherings. The anointing abides within the believer, and it goes where the individual goes. This includes the workplace. God is bringing change to the way we function as a Church. C. Peter Wagner has said the Church is experiencing the greatest change in the way we function as a Body of believers since the Protestant Reformation. That is quite a statement!

One of the changes the Lord is bringing to the Church is our way of thinking about ministry. Believers in the Early Church saw themselves as ministers with a mission. Wherever they went, they shared the good news concerning Jesus. As a result of their zeal and fervent commitment to the Lord, the Church grew rapidly:

> And this took place for two years, so that all who lived in
> Asia heard the word of the Lord, both Jews and Greeks
> (Acts 19:10).

Unfortunately, since the era of the Early Church, the Church's zeal has deteriorated. Compromise and religious rituals, in many cases, have replaced the life of the Spirit in the Church. Although the early believers saw transformation in their cities, the following generations lost the original vision.

As these changes occurred, the Church declined in the exercise of spiritual power. One of the reasons for this decline was that individuals were put in positions of authority in the Church to perform religious tasks. These people came to be known as the clergy. Average church members were discouraged from reading or studying the Scriptures on their own; these churchgoers became known as the laity. For centuries now there has been a division in the Church between clergy and laity, with the clergy doing the work of the Church, while the vast majority of the laity have been relatively ineffective, uninvolved spectators.

Bill Hamon writes about this situation in *The Eternal Church*:

> There were very few copies of the Scriptures available for the everyday professing Christian to study. These people were at the mercy of the Church leaders concerning whether they received truth or error, life or death, reality or religion, and whether they were made a living stone in the living Spiritual Church or were made a cut-and-dried brick in the lifeless Structural Church.[1]

The dictionary defines "clergy" as "persons ordained for religious service; ministers, priests, rabbis, etc."[2] "Laity" is defined as "all the people not included among the clergy."[3]

Rich Marshall explains the difference in his book *God at Work*:

> In most cases when we used the word "clergy," it was referring to those who had responded to a call of God in their lives and were serving Him in a "professional" capacity.

Usually it would mean they were ordained and drew a part, if not all, of their means of livelihood from funds derived through "professional" ministry sources. These clergy types could be pastors, missionaries, church staff, Bible teachers, theologians, leaders in a variety of Christian organizations or any of a number of other possibilities. But whatever the specific assignment, it was pretty clear, they were the "clergy."

"Laity," on the other hand, referred to Christians who were not in the "professional ministry," and the implication was that if they had a call from God, it was not as high a call as the one to "ministry." It did not matter how committed they were to Christ, how much time or money they gave to Christian causes or even how gifted they were in the gifts of the Spirit, or in ministry gifts; they were the "laity."[4]

Today there are a number of ministers and believers in the marketplace who are suddenly coming to a realization: The old paradigm of the clergy doing all the work while the laity watches is just not biblical. In both the Old and New Testaments, God purposed for His people—*all* His people, not just those wearing a collar—to be ministers of reconciliation (see 2 Cor. 5:18-20). God is once again calling us to that task, and a new breed of believers, who see their workplace as their mission field, are responding.

CALLED TO BE WORLD CHANGERS

I am always amazed when I hear people say they have a call from God on their lives for the mission field, and in the next breath, they tell me how they are waiting for the day when they can leave their jobs and go to the mission field. When I question them about what they are doing now, they tell me they are waiting until God opens the door to ministry.

Your mission field may be your neighborhood, school or place of employment.

In the interim, these people are working for a paycheck and doing nothing in the way of ministry. I generally explain to them that they have already found their mission field. Their mission field may be their neighborhood, school or place of employment. The neighborhood, as well as the marketplace, is full of people from every nation who do not know God's saving grace.

These are days of great transition for the Church. If we are going to bring in a harvest of souls and see revival come, we must change the way we think and the way we function as a Church. To a large extent, the Church has been ineffective in reaching the masses of people around us, but a change of seasons is taking place.

Whenever we enter a new season, things may look the same for a period of time. I remember the change from summer to fall in Dallas a couple of years ago. It had been a record-breaking summer—temperatures reached 100 degrees in May. By November we were still having temperatures in the upper 90s. One day, while observing the leaves on the trees, we noticed something strange: Half the leaves were green, and half were red. We laughed as we made the observation, "Even the trees don't know which season it is."

Whenever we move into a new season, it takes time for the fullness of that new season to emerge. For a period of time, the new season looks just like the old, and that is what is happening now in the Church. We try to use old methods for reaching the lost in this new season, and it just won't work.

Dale has a knack for repairing TVs. He has always loved working with wires and anything electrical. After we had pastored for a period of time, several people in the congregation learned of Dale's ability. It was not long before one of the rooms at our house was full of broken television sets. Dale tried for weeks, but he could not fix one of those TVs. Needless to say, he was quite frustrated. After spending some time in prayer to see why he was unable to do what had always been so easy for him, the Lord spoke: "I have not called you to be a TV repairman." Wow! What a revelation! Now Dale understood that he was in a new season in his life. God wanted to do something new with him. Therefore, methods that had worked in the last season would not work in this one. If Dale had not had this frustrating experience, he might never have moved forward in what God had for him at the present time.

It is the same way in the Church. In recent years, we have held evangelistic crusades and numerous revival meetings at churches. Hundreds of programs designed to reach the lost have been implemented. Yet little of this has made a significant difference in reaching the lost and unchurched. The reason these efforts have not been successful is that we have never fully equipped and released most of the believers in our churches. We have not tapped into a powerful resource given by God: His people who are stationed in the marketplace.

In this new season, we must not continue using only the old methods for reaching the harvest. New methods of reaching the world must be embraced by those in church ministry and those who have a marketplace anointing. Only then will we see the harvest come into the kingdom of God.

Finding businesspeople in the Bible who impacted their world is easy.

- Abraham was a notably wealthy businessman. God used him to demonstrate a life of faith in a God who can cause the impossible to become possible.
- Moses was another remarkably successful businessman. His leadership skills were evident when he led an entire nation out of bondage in Egypt.
- Nehemiah was a government worker in the king's palace. He eventually became a governor and was sent to Jerusalem to help rebuild the city wall. Nehemiah mobilized an entire city to accomplish in a few days that which had not been done in more than 100 years.
- Lydia apparently was a prosperous merchant who sold royal purple cloth to the rich. Her home was opened up as a ministry center for Paul and Silas.

These are only a few of the men and women God used in the marketplace of their society.

Men and women around the world are gifted by God to reach their societies. One of these people is a man living in Quilmes, a city near Buenos Aires, Argentina. Carlos Annacondia has been a key figure in the revival in Argentina for the past 15 years. He is a businessman with a marketplace anointing. Annacondia is not a seminary-trained clergyman; he operates a factory that makes nuts and bolts. Nevertheless, he holds massive evangelistic meetings and moves in a powerful demonstration of signs, wonders and miracles. Annacondia openly confronts demonic powers. People are healed and lives are dramatically changed under his ministry. He has been instrumental in helping to change his nation and is helping to change other nations.

God will use whatever we offer to Him. Some people do not go to an office or factory each day, but they do live in neighborhoods full of people. Our homes can be offered as places where the presence and anointing of God is released. The book of Acts shows the New Testament pattern for reaching a city through homes. There we find reports of many miracles and salvations that occurred outside a church building:

- The Holy Spirit fell on those gathered in the upper room of a house (see Acts 2:1-4).
- A multitude gathered in the streets when they heard people speaking in tongues (see Acts 2:6).
- The Church grew as a result of the believers worshiping and fellowshipping from house to house (see Acts 2:46,47).
- A lame man was healed at the entrance to the Temple and gained the attention of the crowd (see Acts 3:1-10).
- A lame man at Lystra was healed (see Acts 14:8-10).
- Lydia and her household received salvation at a meeting beside a river (see Acts 16:13-15).
- Salvation came to a jailer and his household when he saw the power of God open the prison doors (see Acts 16:27-33).

Releasing of the anointing in a home can bring change into a city. Frank Damazio encourages believers to use their homes for reaching a city:

The household approach to city reaching is certainly a New Testament model and one that will work mightily in the twenty-first century. Paul's city-reaching approach involved laypeople and the home, or the household. In Romans 16, Paul lists his many coworkers in Christ; these were people who, for the most part, opened their homes. Their homes became houses of Holy Spirit activity—what I call "ministry centers."[5]

Believers are called to be world changers. They are God's ambassadors to the people around them. These ambassadors have an anointing to reach their neighborhoods and places of employment. The giftings released through the marketplace anointing will be used by God to expand His kingdom. God's Holy Spirit will equip people to minister His power, whether in the home, a place of business or wherever God's people may be.

God will also release finances to implement the tasks that need to be performed. Finances are not the only gift of those in the marketplace, but they are a necessary gift. In the same way that God gave people like Abraham, Jacob and Moses an ability to gain wealth, he can do the same thing today. These men used their wealth to bring forth God's purposes on the earth. An anointing is available to release wealth so God's purposes can come forth today.

Recently, my friend Chuck Pierce took a team around the world to pray for the unlocking of finances. The team recognized that a poverty mentality has operated in the Church for too long. It takes money to do what needs to be done if world evangelization is going to occur: "But you shall remember the LORD your God, for it is He who is giving you power to make wealth, that He may confirm His covenant which He swore to your fathers, as it is this day" (Deut. 8:18). The team went to several major cities where wealth had been withheld in the past. These cities included Chicago, London, Frankfurt, Berlin, Warsaw, Zurich and Singapore.

Chuck and his team prayed over each city at strategic sites and performed prophetic acts of intercession.[6] During the prayer journey, reports came in about financial and other break-throughs. Jane Hansen, president of Aglow International, reported that the organization had been very low on funds. But after Jane had sent an appeal letter and called for a day of fasting and prayer among her staff, the staff took up an offering for the ministry of $7,500. Soon after, they received a phone call with a $250,000 commitment to the ministry.

Another lady needed $100 to attend a class where she worked. As she prayed and read the report about this trip, faith swelled up in her heart. She decided to trust God for the need. She received $250! God is unlocking finances for the advancing of His purposes. The marketplace anointing will unlock finances to advance the gospel throughout the world.

Those with a marketplace anointing often find themselves leading or participating in Bible studies, prayer groups or times of ministry in the workplace. Tiffany Ramsey is one of those people. In *A People of Destiny*, I tell the story of this young woman who works for a telecommunications company. Tiffany is an excellent employee and sees the marketplace as her mission field. After several requests from other employees who recognized there was something different about Tiffany, she received permission to begin a Bible study at work during the lunch hour. People began attending and were hungering for more of the Lord. Additional meetings were added during the week to meet the needs of those wanting prayer and teaching from the Word. Coworkers have been receiving Jesus as their Savior, becoming filled with the Holy Spirit and experiencing healing and deliverance. The group has grown and is now a company-recognized employee special-interest group known as Ambassadors for Christ. Representatives of companies in other cities have contacted Tiffany to learn how to start similar groups where they work.

A harvest of souls is ready to come into the kingdom of God. But it will take the entire Body of Christ, using the giftings and anointings given by the Lord, to facilitate this. A marketplace anointing is being released today upon men and women. Our familiar way of functioning in church is changing. No longer do we wait for a church service to lead a person to salvation. No longer do we wait for a professional minister to pray for someone to be healed. No longer do we live one way in church and another way at work.

God has put a marketplace anointing on His people to advance His purposes on the earth. Wherever His people go, signs, wonders and miracles follow them. May the history books record the effect of this group of men and women in the same way Luke recorded the work of believers in the Early Church: "These men who have upset the world have come here also" (Acts 17:6).

DISCUSSION QUESTIONS

1. Discuss what happened after the era of the Early Church that caused much of the Church to move away from life in the Spirit.
2. Describe the traditional thinking concerning clergy. Describe the traditional thinking concerning the laity.
3. What are some of the more traditional ways of evangelizing? Have you ever participated in those methods? What were the results?
4. Tell about some of the businesspeople found in the Bible. How did God use them?
5. How were homes in the Bible used to reach people and cities?

6. Why are finances necessary to advance God's kingdom?

7. What are some ways God can use businesspeople in the marketplace?

8. How can God use you in the mission field where He has placed you at the present time?

Chapter Nine

Revival Anointing

"Look at this!" Sharon cried, running through the church and waving a piece of paper. "Danny's eyes are healed!" Her face beamed as she shared the doctor's report with anyone who would listen.

GOD'S HEART TO HEAL

Only a couple of weeks before, Dale and I had had a conversation with Danny and his mother, Sharon. Dale had noticed that Danny's glasses were badly scratched and should be replaced. As their pastor, he was concerned, and he explained to Sharon that she should consider getting another pair of glasses for Danny.

Sharon made the appointment with the eye doctor. Before going to the doctor's office, she brought Danny by the church so Dale could pray with him. She had learned that healing is in the atonement. Jesus died not only for our salvation but also so that we can be healed.

Dale spent several minutes talking with eight-year-old Danny. During that time he prayed silently, *How should we pray? What do*

You want me to pray for this young man? Dale realized it was not enough to pray simply from what he knew about the situation; he desired to know what was on the Lord's heart to pray. After sharing some of the promises of the Lord for healing found in God's Word, Dale felt impressed to ask Danny to do something.

"Danny, let's pray and ask the Lord to forgive all the other children who have made fun of you for wearing glasses. Can you think of the names of the people who have mocked you and called you names because you wear glasses?"

"Yes," Danny replied. "I can remember lots of them."

"Pray with me," Dale encouraged him. "Father, I know you are a God who heals. I come to you today asking you to heal my eyes. I realize there are people who have hurt me. They have ridiculed me because I wear glasses."

Danny repeated each sentence after Dale. Finally, Dale told Danny, "Now begin to name the people who have hurt you. Let the Lord know you are forgiving them."

"Lord, these are the people who have hurt me," Danny prayed. "Jessie, Wayne, Justin, Charles, Andy . . ." Tears streamed down Danny's face as he acknowledged his forgiveness toward each one. After what seemed an endless list of names, Dale led Danny in a prayer, asking the Lord to forgive him for his hate and anger toward the other boys.

"Lord, now I ask you to heal Danny's eyes," Dale prayed. "In the same way that you have healed his heart, I ask you to heal his eyes."

Danny and his mother left for the doctor's office. She sensed the Lord had done a work of restoration in Danny's heart, and this was more important than healing his eyes.

On Sunday morning, Sharon hurried into the church with the report. "The doctor was surprised when he checked Danny's eyes," she announced. "He couldn't understand what had happened since the visit three months ago. The glasses Danny had worn were very thick. Now, the doctor says Danny doesn't need *new* glasses—he doesn't need *any* glasses! His eyes are healed!"

SIGNS, WONDERS AND MIRACLES

How astonished and surprised we are when the Lord performs a miracle like this! Yet God planned for signs, wonders and miracles to be the norm in the lives of Christians:

> Most Christians fail to find fulfillment in experiencing the Holy Spirit's empowerment for ministry. In reality, far too many of God's children function below the potential available to them. They have accepted an *ordinary* walk with the Lord when He has made the *extraordinary* available. The heavenly dynamic of signs and wonders can operate *naturally* through the believer and release him or her into *supernatural* manifestations of the life and works of Jesus.[1]

According to 2 Peter 1:4, through God's glory and His goodness, He "has granted to us His precious and magnificent promises, in order that by them [we] might become partakers of the divine nature." Verses 5-7 of that same chapter show that God desires His character to be manifest in His children. He gives us His Holy Spirit, and His Holy Spirit gives us the power to become the people He wants us to be and to perform His will on the earth. As God's children, we are to look and act like our Father:

> Beloved, now we are children of God, and it has not appeared as yet what we shall be. We know that, when He appears, we shall be like Him, because we shall see Him just as He is (1 John 3:2).

Kevin is a toddler who closely resembles his father. He has the same red hair; his pictures look like the baby pictures of his father. However, it is not exclusively the looks that are similar. Kevin loves to walk around in his father's shoes. He pretends he is doing the same things he sees his father doing. He will stand in front of a mirror and pretend he is shaving his face. He pushes his toy lawnmower just like he sees his dad do when he's mowing the lawn. Kevin has his father's nature in him. Therefore, he wants to be and act like his father.

A young eagle is the same way. When a baby eagle is born, it eats, breathes and thinks like the parent eagle. Later in life, the growing bird will spread its wings and soar above the cliffs. The reason the young eagle can do this is because it is the child of the parent eagle. It does not crawl like a worm or live on the ground like a lion or tiger. That is the not the nature of an eagle. It flies because it is the natural thing for an eagle to do. It does all the things the parent eagle does.

Likewise, God created His children to become more and more like Jesus, both in likeness and in character. Because Jesus performed signs, wonders and miracles by the Spirit of God and according to the Father's will, He now invites his brethren, the children of God, to do the same kinds of works, even "greater works" (John 14:12).

Behold, I and the children whom the LORD has given me are for signs and wonders in Israel from the LORD of hosts, who dwells on Mount Zion (Isa. 8:18).

THE FRUIT AND THE GIFTS

As I mentioned, for a period of time I wrestled with whether I wanted the fruit or the gifts of the Spirit in my life. I was amazed when I discovered I could have both! The Lord desires His children to operate in the fullness of the gifts of the Spirit. The gifts are to flow freely, along with the fruit of the Spirit. Only then will we look and act like Jesus.

Signs and wonders are as old as the Bible itself. They are prevalent throughout the history of mankind, including both the Old Testament and the New Testament. As we have seen, God loaned His supernatural power to certain Old Testament people, enabling them for specific tasks. After they performed the task, the Spirit of God would lift from them.

The gifts of the Spirit are new since the Day of Pentecost, but the power behind them is the same. In the New Testament, Jesus and the Father sent the Holy Spirit, and the center of operations for God's Spirit changed from heaven to Earth. The move occurred as the result of the indwelling of God's Spirit in the lives of believers. The Holy Spirit now operates in and through the believer in Christ.

In the Old Testament, the Holy Spirit came mightily *upon* men and women for definite assignments. Today, the Holy Spirit dwells mightily *within* men and women. In the Old Testament, men *experienced* divine power. Since New Testament times, men have *received* power.

DISCERNMENT

It is important to remember that not everything supernatural is from God. Satan is also able to manifest supernatural power, although his power is vastly inferior to God's. Nevertheless, discernment is necessary to know the difference between manifestations of God's power and Satan's power.

Believers *can* be deceived. Deception implies a misrepresentation of facts—an attempt to make someone believe that which is not true. Jesus warned His followers not to be taken in by false signs and wonders:

> For many will come in My name, saying, "I am the Christ," and will mislead many. . . . For false Christs and false prophets will arise and will show great signs and wonders, so as to mislead, if possible, even the elect (Matt. 24:5,24).

Even sincere Christians can be deceived, or Jesus would not have warned against it. Fortunately, one of the gifts the Holy Spirit provides allows us to discern the false from the true (see 1 Cor. 12:10). Discerning of spirits is a gift required for distinguishing counterfeit spirits.

There are three basic types of discernment. The first is *natural,* often referred to as common sense. Natural discernment belongs to both the Christian and non-Christian. We operate in this realm when we pass judgment on people, circumstances or behavior. The teaching received in our homes and the effect of our environment and culture cause us to judge whether something is good or bad. A person taught to be honest and to tell the truth will judge it wrong to lie. His conscience will constrain him when he is tempted to be dishonest. Even non-Christians can be taught, by their parents or the culture, to be honest. The secular world uses this type of discernment as a basis for many of its decisions. Since this type is not necessarily based on the Word of God, it can be unreliable.

The second type of discernment is intellectual, what I like to call *renewed-mind* discernment. A mind that is renewed in Christ operates in this dimension of discernment. Renewed-mind discernment grows as we get to know God and His Word:

> For everyone who partakes only of milk is not accustomed to the word of righteousness, for he is a babe. But solid

food is for the mature, who because of practice have their senses trained to discern good and evil (Heb. 5:13,14).

The word "senses" here refers to perceptions or judgments. As we mature spiritually, we will immediately be able to recognize when something is not right. We should be able to recognize that which does not line up with the truth of God's Word.

A lady named Rita once asked me to look at a necklace she had purchased overseas. The jewelry reminded her of the country she had visited, and Rita truly enjoyed wearing it and showing it to her friends. However, soon after she began wearing it, she also began to experience periods of depression and mental torment. At the same time, she was growing in the Lord and having her mind renewed by the Word, and she found herself feeling more and more uncomfortable about wearing the necklace. As I inspected the necklace, I noticed engravings of temples of false religions around the edges of the stones. When I pointed these out to her, she said she had been disturbed by these etchings.

Rita had purchased the necklace shortly after becoming a Christian. At the time she thought the temples were simply representative of the culture in the country she was visiting. Since then, she had taken part in Bible studies and had grown in her knowledge of the Word. She no longer viewed the temples as simply cultural but instead saw them as having spiritual significance. Not wanting to appear flaky or as a "demon chaser," she came to me seeking counsel.

When, at my suggestion, Rita disposed of the necklace, the bouts of oppression and depression subsided. Her joy returned, and she felt "normal" again. Rita's uncomfortable feeling when wearing the necklace had actually been renewed-mind discernment in action.

Renewed-mind discernment enables us to identify the counterfeit of the supernatural, or anything supernatural that does not come from God. As Christians we may be the objects of attacks and persecution that seem out of proportion to the normal difficulties of life. With renewed-mind discernment in operation, we can discern the source of these attacks and persecution. Sometimes curses or overt occult activity will be directed at believers. Occult activity is not a figment of people's imaginations, nor are curses things of the past or of faraway cultures, as evidenced by the following story.

I once ministered to a man who had been involved in Satanism. He told me that one of his assignments had been to go into churches in his city for the purpose of destroying them. He did two things to accomplish this task. First, he released curses of strife and division against the members of the church. Then he released curses of divorce against the pastor. Before long, the congregation would begin to engage in gossip, strife and division; and the pastor would experience marital problems. It didn't take long for attendance to drop and the church to shut down. Several churches had closed, possibly as a result of his infiltration.

This same man told me he had *not* been effective in the church where I was ministering to him because of the depth of unity in that church. His curses were powerless: "Like a sparrow in its flitting, like a swallow in its flying, so a curse without cause does not alight" (Prov. 26:2). Such spiritual attacks may also require a greater level of intercession and spiritual warfare to successfully ward off the persecution.

The third type of discernment is the *discerning of spirits*. We find this gift listed in 1 Corinthians 12. Discerning, or distinguishing, spirits is a gift of the Holy Spirit that gives us insight into the spirit world. A person with this gift is able to discern more than just evil spirits; he or she can discern the presence of God, the Holy Spirit and heavenly angels. There are times when we may sense the presence of God in a meeting. Discerning of spirits is operating at that time.

Discerning spirits will equip Christians to be aware of false signs and wonders. The fact that demons perform these false signs and wonders causes some Christians to reject signs and wonders altogether. However, we must avoid the temptation to throw out the baby with the bathwater. The true supernatural power of God must not be eschewed simply because we hear of the counterfeit operating elsewhere.

> We must not disdain the true supernatural power of God simply because we hear its counterfeit is operating elsewhere.

One obvious way to tell the difference between a counterfeit miracle and a genuine one is by asking ourselves *Who gets the glory for this miracle?* Another important question is *What is the doctrine of salvation being taught here?* Some religions teach that we must earn our way to heaven. However, it is faith in the finished work of Jesus that purchases our salvation; it is not earned through our good works (see Eph. 2:8,9). But we don't stop teaching the true way to salvation just because some religions teach a false doctrine. And we don't stop demonstrating true signs and wonders just because the enemy manifests the false.

LEARNING BY EXAMPLE

The dawn of the twentieth century saw a fresh release of Holy Spirit power that continues today. The Body of Christ is experiencing a fresh outpouring by the Spirit. Current signs and wonders are gaining attention worldwide, both within the Church and in the secular world.

Signs, wonders and miracles were part of Jesus' ministry. He healed the woman with the issue of blood whom doctors had not been able to cure (see Luke 8:43,44). He healed a man born blind (see John 9:2-7). He healed many people with a variety of sicknesses and diseases:

> And while the sun was setting, all who had any sick with various diseases brought them to Him; and laying His hands on every one of them, He was healing them (Luke 4:40).

Jesus also cast out demons. Deliverance was a common characteristic of His ministry. He ministered to the man in the synagogue with an unclean spirit (see Mark 1:23-26). The man had probably been attending the synagogue for many years. Demons can hide in a religious atmosphere where there is no power. However, when the presence of the Lord came in, the demon could no longer hide. Jesus rebuked the demon and set the man free.

Another time, Jesus set a demoniac free so the man's mind was restored (see Mark 5:2-15). Many people today need the same delivering power to free them from sickness, uncleanness and tormented minds.

Jesus was able to raise the dead during His ministry on Earth. He raised the daughter of Jairus from her deathbed (see Luke 8:52-55). He raised Lazarus from death (see John 11:14,43,44). He did not raise every person who died, but sometimes it was not the Father's will for a person to die. In those situations, Jesus exercised power over premature death.

Jesus operated in prophecy and the word of knowledge, other gifts listed in 1 Corinthians 12. He prophesied about things to come. We see this in John 1:47 when He spoke about Nathaniel. He even prophesied regarding His own death (see Matt. 20:18,19).

Jesus demonstrated miraculous signs. He sent Peter to get money from the mouth of a fish to pay their taxes (see Matt. 17:27). He turned water to wine at a wedding (see John 2:7-9). He spoke to a storm and calmed the wind and the sea (see Matt. 8:26).

The apostles also operated in signs and wonders. Healing was a regular part of their ministry (see Acts 3:6-8; 5:12; 9:33,34). They even raised the dead (see Acts 9:36-41). The same power that empowered Jesus flowed through the apostles:

> At the hands of the apostles many signs and wonders were taking place among the people; and they were all with one accord in Solomon's portico (Acts 5:12).

Believers in the Early Church were also empowered by the Holy Spirit to perform signs and wonders (see Heb. 2:4).

Jesus desires to continue His ministry today through the hands of His children, whom He purchased with His blood through the sacrifice on the Cross:

> Truly, truly, I say to you, he who believes in Me, the works that I do shall he do also; and greater works than these shall he do; because I go to the Father (John 14:12).

Signs and wonders release a revival anointing to bring in a harvest of souls. Recently I was ministering in a church where we worshiped the Lord and sang songs about the "river of God." While we were singing, I sensed the Lord wanted to release a fresh baptism on the people because there were enemies He wanted to drown in the water. Among these enemies were discouragement, grief, fear and hopelessness. After getting permission from the pastor, I instructed the congregation. The ministry team lined up at the front with glasses of water in their hands. The people who were beset by these enemies passed in front of the ministry team, and as we sprinkled water on the people, God set them free.

As we sprinkled water on those people, the power of God was released. Many fell under the power of the Spirit. Some shouted. Some danced. People were gloriously set free from enemies:

> Then the lame will leap like a deer, and the tongue of the dumb will shout for joy. For waters will break forth in the wilderness and streams in the Arabah (Isa. 35:6).

We find these types of signs and wonders throughout the Bible, including examples of weak human bodies being affected gloriously by the manifest presence of God (see Exod. 40:35; 2 Chron. 7:2; Matt. 28:4; Acts 2:15,16; 9:3,4; Eph. 5:18; Rev. 1:17).

In the midst of the signs and wonders flowing that night, a young lady rushed to the front of the church. "This is God! This is God!" she cried out. "How do I get Jesus into my heart?"

Historically, revival has been accompanied by the supernatural manifestations of the Holy Spirit. Signs and wonders were an ordinary part of Smith Wigglesworth's life. Wigglesworth (1859-1947) was a plumber, but the power of God enabled him to heal the sick, deliver the captives and raise the dead. John G. Lake (1870-1935), an apostle to Africa, had the ability to produce faith in others that resulted in healings of a startling nature. Mel Tari, a contemporary world evangelist from Indonesia, has reported many signs and wonders done by the power of the Spirit in his home country.

The late John Wimber, founder of the Vineyard Association of Churches, described the necessity of signs and wonders in reaching many regions of the world today:

When the gospel first penetrates a region, if we don't go in with an understanding of and use of the supernatural power of the Holy Spirit, we just don't make much headway. . . . The way the gospel is spreading there are confrontations, healings, miracles, signs and wonders.[2]

After the crucifixion Jesus walked with His disciples on the road to Emmaus. He opened their minds so they could understand the Scriptures. That same Jesus will walk in our midst today by the power of the Holy Spirit. He will open our minds and hearts to the reality of signs and wonders in the lives of believers (see Luke 24:13-35). The promise of the Lord is for signs and wonders to manifest through our lives in order to demonstrate the kingdom of God:

These signs will accompany those who have believed: in My name they will cast out demons, they will speak with new tongues; they will pick up serpents, and if they drink any deadly poison, it shall not hurt them; they will lay hands on the sick, and they will recover (Mark 16:17,18).

We must allow a revival anointing to flow through us in order to reap a harvest of souls!

DISCUSSION QUESTIONS

1. Discuss the difference between the fruit of the Spirit and the gifts of the Spirit.
2. What is deception? Name the three types of deception. Give an example of each.

3. Tell why you believe a Christian can or cannot be deceived.

4. What is "discerning of spirits"?

5. What were some of the signs and wonders present in the ministry of Jesus? In the lives of the apostles? In the Early Church?

6. Describe some of the signs and wonders you have seen.

7. How can signs and wonders be used to release a harvest of souls for the kingdom of God?

8. Are you willing to let the Lord use you for signs and wonders?

Chapter Ten

True and False Anointings

I will never forget that day. A person parading as a minister of the Lord had been exposed. Rather than being a genuine minister of the Lord Jesus, this person was, in fact, a charlatan.

For some time I had been troubled over what had been happening, as this person had continued to gain favor with Christian leaders throughout the nation. Powerful signs and wonders were present in her meetings. Few people questioned her practices. Those who did were warned not to judge or they could come under the judgment of God. I happened to be one of those who openly expressed my concern in spite of the warnings.

Not only was I concerned, but I also felt a responsibility to alert anyone who would listen to me, including pastors, leaders and believers. Very few, however, were willing to listen. After all, those who hosted this minister had large, powerful meetings. Who was I to question what others were endorsing? The signs and wonders were so powerful. Not only that, but the minister seemed so sincere and godly in conduct. How could this not be from God?

I asked the pastors and leaders if they could give me a scriptural defense for these supernatural manifestations. The only verse I was given was Acts 2:19:

> And I will grant wonders in the sky above, and signs on
> the earth beneath, blood, and fire, and vapor of smoke.

One such discussion was held at a church where I was ministering. The minister in question was scheduled to speak at this church at a later time. I decided to ask the pastor about the validity of applying Acts 2:19 to this person's ministry.

"That is not what that scripture is talking about, is it?" I asked the pastor.

"No," he replied. "That is not what it means."

Yet as we continued the discussion, he assured me of this person's godly character. Still, I felt compelled to urge him not to allow her to come to his church. "It does not matter what her character looks like," I pleaded. "These manifestations are from Satan."

In one of her meetings, people were told to close their eyes and worship God. While their eyes were closed and the people were worshiping, the speaker pulled feathers from a handkerchief in her sleeve. When the congregation opened their eyes, feathers were floating in the air. They were told that the feathers were the Holy Spirit.

Now a minister had caught the whole thing on video, proving she was a fraud. The charlatan had been deceiving sincere, hungry believers.

SUSCEPTIBLE TO FALSE SIGNS AND WONDERS

Prior to the time these evil practices were uncovered, I was not the only person expressing concern. Many others had discerned the work of the enemy and were warning people to stay away from this ministry. Yet few were willing to listen. Why were many not heeding the warnings?

One reason people are susceptible to false signs and wonders is that mankind was destined for the supernatural. God is spirit, and He put within each person a desire to be like his or her Creator. Men and women long for an encounter with God's power, and when they don't find it in the Church, they look elsewhere, reaching out for that which looks like God's power. If we are not able to discern the source of power behind the manifestations, we can be deceived.

Another reason we are easy prey for those who perform false signs and wonders is that many Christians are frankly bored. They have heard the biblical teaching about God's power. They can sing the songs, quote the Scriptures and pray long prayers. But they are bored with life as usual in the Church. Nothing seems to change. They go through all the right religious rituals and practices but never experience the supernatural power they have read about, sung about and prayed about. They have become complacent and are no longer spiritually alert.

A third reason Christians can be deceived by false supernatural phenomena is a lack of knowledge. Many believers have little understanding of the Bible and how to apply its principles to everyday life. George Barna expresses this concern in *The Habits of Highly Effective Churches*, explaining that Christians don't know the content of their faith and show little concern about their ignorance. Barna says that this lack of spiritual knowledge and wisdom has resulted in a Body of believers who are both incapable of applying their faith in daily circumstances and unable to persuasively share their faith with those who so desperately need it:

> The problem, of course, is not that the Christian faith
> does not have the answers people need to life's challenges;

the problem is that most Christians do not devote anything but a spare minute here and there to grappling with the underpinnings and personal implications of Christian theology. Most churches seem to have acquiesced to people's determination to paint a happy face on their Bible and to keep all teaching and related discussions about faith matters at an elementary level.[1]

DOCTRINES OF DEMONS

Christians need a solid foundation in the Bible to help them discern supernatural manifestations. After all, false supernatural manifestations are nothing new. Similar practices can be found throughout history:

> During the Dark Ages, people claimed to possess genuine splinters of the cross that Jesus died on at Golgotha; that was when some claimed to own some of the real blood of Jesus and kept it in little bottles as a relic of the Lord; some said they owned straw from Jesus' original manger; pieces of His garments; and yes, believe it or not, during the Dark Ages, some even claimed to possess "feathers" that were accidentally dropped by the Holy Spirit. These were called "relics of the Holy Spirit."
>
> These kinds of tricks are always easy to pander on people who are unfounded in God's Word. As Hosea 4:6 says, "My people are destroyed for lack of knowledge." It is easy to pull tricks off on people who are not educated in God's Word. They have no sense of discernment.[2]

Believers also need the power of the Holy Spirit. In the Old Testament, when the high priest wanted to know the mind and counsel of God, he used the Urim and Thummim. No one knows for certain what these objects were. Some Bible translators give the meanings of these words as "lights" and "perfections," which are also biblical descriptions of God's Word and the Holy Spirit's enlightening us.

Believers need the Spirit of God and the Word of God to know the mind and counsel of the Lord. A knowledge of the Bible and a discerning of spirits by the power of the Holy Spirit will help guard believers against deception. Discerning of spirits is a weapon for spiritual warfare to guard against deception. By its operation, we can know the source of power behind any manifestation.

Two great deceptions Christians are warned against are lying signs and wonders and the doctrines of devils, or demons. The magicians of pharaoh reproduced the signs God gave Moses. Nonetheless, there came a time when the magicians could no longer counterfeit God's power. Their failure forced them to acknowledge, "This is the finger of God" (Exod. 8:19).

There is a warning in Deuteronomy concerning prophets, or dreamers of dreams. When such a person rises in the midst of God's people, spiritual discernment is needed:

> If a prophet or a dreamer of dreams arises among you and gives you a sign or a wonder, and the sign or the wonder comes true, concerning which he spoke to you, saying, "Let us go after other gods (whom you have not known) and let us serve them," you shall not listen to the words of that prophet or that dreamer of dreams; for the LORD your God is testing you to find out if you love the LORD your God with all your heart and with all your soul (Deut. 13:1-3).

No matter how powerful the manifestations, if a prophet or dreamer leads people away from the one true God revealed in

Scripture, he or she is a false prophet. We are not to be naïve; we are to test the spirits to learn the source of their supernatural power.

Christians are also cautioned to be alert to doctrines of devils:

> But the Spirit explicitly says that in later times some will fall away from the faith, paying attention to deceitful spirits and doctrines of demons (1 Tim. 4:1).

Doctrines of demons are teachings designed to deceive believers and lead them away from simple faith in the Lord Jesus Christ.

I remember listening to a tape given to me by someone who wanted me to check out the teaching of a particular minister. The man doing the teaching seemed well grounded in the Bible. He started his sermon by laying a good foundation from the Word of God. At first, I was impressed. However, as I continued listening, I realized he had taken a turn from the truth of the Bible. The more he taught, the farther he departed from the truth. I could hear in the background the response of the people at the meeting: They cheered, they shouted and they clapped. The more he taught, the more enthusiastic they became. He ended by making a startling statement: "Just think. The time will come when every person you have ever prayed for will get saved. Even the devil himself will eventually be saved." The applause, cheering and shouting from the audience sounded as if it could take the roof off!

The people had heard what they wanted to hear. God's Word warns us about those types of teachings:

> For the time will come when they will not endure sound doctrine; but wanting to have their ears tickled, they will accumulate for themselves teachers in accordance to

their own desires, and will turn away their ears from the truth and will turn aside to myths (2 Tim. 4:3,4).

I had just listened to the doctrine of demons—a teaching designed by Satan to deceive God's people and turn them away from simple faith in the Lord Jesus Christ. The teacher was even using Greek and Hebrew words to validate what he was teaching. It all sounded so convincing. How thankful I was that I had a solid foundation in the Word of God! Without this foundation I, too, could have been deceived.

THE SOULISH NATURE

Satan can counterfeit the true anointing of God's Spirit—but only to a degree. Like the magicians of Pharaoh, there is a limit to what he is able to do. As we fill our minds with the Word of God and our hearts with the Spirit of God, we will be able to discern Satan's false anointing.

Studying *everything* about the enemy is not essential in order to recognize his workings. We need to major in the truth. When people are trained to recognize counterfeit money, they do not spend their time studying the false bills. They spend most of their time focusing on genuine money. Therefore, when counterfeit money comes along, they are able to recognize it immediately. It is the same with the anointing.

People who attempt to imitate God's anointing using their own fleshly methods are drawing on Satan's power and resources, whether they know it or not. The manifestations that occur in these situations are not from God's Spirit but rather from a soulish nature. The soul is the seat of man's will and personality. It involves the mind, will and emotions. Even a Christian can operate from the soul rather than from God's Spirit.

So often we hear people say, "I *feel* the presence of the Lord." If we are not careful, we can interpret feelings as being valid proof of God's presence or anointing. Yet our feelings often prove to be unreliable, as evidenced in the Scriptures:

- Feelings can tell us we are alone, but the Bible says God will never leave or forsake us (see Heb. 13:5).
- Feelings can tell us we are unloved, though God's Word says He loves us (see 1 John 4:7).
- Feelings can tell us we are guilty, but the Lord says He has forgiven us (see Rev. 12:10,11).

Feelings come from our soulish nature. A person who *feels* spiritual may choose to prophesy. When that individual doesn't feel spiritual, he won't prophesy. That individual may be operating out of a natural ability and not the anointing of God. We can, however, operate in the anointing of God and still have feelings; otherwise, we would be like dead people. But we are not led by our feelings—only by an anointing from the Holy Spirit.

Sometimes, when we are operating in the power of the Holy Spirit, our feelings do get involved. Our emotions should not be interpreted as a sign of the anointing, however. Emotions are a product of the soul and not a guarantee of the anointing of the Holy Spirit.

People operating out of natural abilities tend to have powerful personalities. Evidence suggests that individuals who possess high levels of energy and drive or those who tend to have a positive mood can become great leaders. They tend to be more interpersonal in their relationships. The energetic personalities of these individuals infuse excitement and energy into others. They have the ability to create vision, and they possess the capacity to design a strategy that leads to the implementation of the vision.[3] These people are able to sway audiences to their way of thinking.

Motivational speakers often have this type of powerful personality, and they are in great demand. Power is released through them to influence their audiences toward a particular goal. Watchman Nee cautions believers to recognize the difference between a natural charisma and a true anointing of the Holy Spirit:

> Let us remember that all works done through emotion are questionable and transient. In the work done through the power of the Holy Spirit, man does not need to exert his own strength nor do anything by himself. If a work is done by soul strength, one has to exert lots of energy and employ numerous methods such as weeping, shouting, jumping, incessant singing of choruses or the telling of a number of moving stories (I do not say that hymns and stories should not be used, only everything must be done within appropriate bounds). . . . We all know that some individuals have a magnetic attraction about them. Though they may not be fairer or more eloquent than another, they nonetheless can draw people to themselves.[4]

Natural abilities are not necessarily evil. They can, in fact, be positive traits. They become evil only when they are used to deceive believers into thinking they are witnessing the supernatural anointing of the Holy Spirit.

PROTECTION AGAINST DECEPTION

Several safeguards will protect us against deception and help us remain sensitive to the true anointing of God's Holy Spirit. The first way to safeguard against deception is to submit to leaders who walk what they teach. In recognizing the true anointing of the Lord, we should not only examine the source of the manifestations of power, but also look at the lives and character of those who are ministering. I am not speaking of sinless perfection, but I am talking about walking a life that is pleasing to the Lord. We become like those with whom we associate.

Lot participated with Abraham in many of his adventures in faith. Yet Lot later deteriorated into a man with a mind that was nearly reprobate. He had parted ways with Abraham and associated with the ungodly. Many genuine men and women of God start out strong but take a wrong turn at some point. Either because they are not spiritually accountable or do not submit to godly authority, their lives and ministries end up shipwrecked. Such tragedies can be avoided if we will submit ourselves to leaders who live what they teach.

The next safeguard is to walk a balanced life, free of excesses. We need the whole counsel of God to be balanced believers. We require not only the Word of God in our lives, but we also need the Spirit of God. When we neglect either, we become imbalanced. I once heard someone say, "Without the Word, we puff up. Without the Spirit, we dry up."

We must ground ourselves in the Word of God so we may have a plumb line for our lives. The foundation found in Hebrews 6:1,2 is vital for the believer:

> Therefore leaving the elementary teaching about the Christ, let us press on to maturity, not laying again a *foundation of repentance from dead works and of faith toward God, of instruction about washings, and laying on of hands, and the resurrection of the dead, and eternal judgment* (emphasis added).

Books and Bible studies on these topics will help ensure a strong foundation for life. Later, when difficulties, winds of doctrinal change and false ministers arise, the well-grounded believer is able to stand strong.

Another way to guard ourselves is to get deliverance and healing where needed. Many people have experienced hurts, trauma, violence, occult involvement or other forms of wounding. These events can open the door to demonization and/or severe emotional pain. Freedom from these places of pain leaves us more sensitive to the Spirit of God. We can then discern the true from the false with greater accuracy.

Finally, we must live a life of no compromise to sin. Sin hardens the heart; it sears the conscience and makes us insensitive to the promptings of the Holy Spirit. Throughout the Bible we read of individuals chosen by the Lord to do great exploits. But those who allowed sin into their lives gradually moved away from the Lord and His plans for them. Their lives ended with a sad epitaph of being evil before the Lord.

Genuine signs and wonders can be examined and tested. Our youngest son, Mark, was miraculously healed when he was two years old. The doctors could find no medical explanation for his healing. The doctors finally had to admit, "This is a miracle."

Jesus encouraged true miracles to be examined. He told the 10 leprous men to go to the priests and be examined (see Luke 17:11-14). The custom was for the priests to check for any signs of leprosy. If they found nothing, they would declare the leper to be cleansed and healed. We can do the same thing.

Although Satan has a false anointing and people can have natural abilities and strong personalities, God has a true anointing for His people. We must not allow man's natural abilities or the manifestation of false anointing to rob us of the true anointing. Jesus promised that you and I, as His followers, would have access to the anointing of the Holy Spirit.

DISCUSSION QUESTIONS

1. What are some of the reasons believers are susceptible to false signs and wonders?
2. Name two great deceptions Christians are warned against. What are doctrines of devils, or demons?
3. Why is it not necessary to spend a lot of time studying false anointings?
4. Why are feelings unreliable? What part of man do emotions come from?
5. List several safeguards from deception.

Chapter Eleven

Fat-Bull Anointing

Would we ever get there? It seemed as though we had been driving for months, although it had been only three days. But those three days had been filled with indescribable fear, a sick stomach and very little sleep. How I cried out for the Lord to deliver me from the torment I was experiencing!

DELIVERANCE FROM FEAR

My family was driving a missionary family to Guadalajara, Mexico. They had been given a homemade trailer in which to carry their belongings. We were pulling the trailer with our car, while the missionary family drove behind us in theirs. Each time our car reached a speed of 45 miles per hour, the trailer wobbled from side to side. Our car felt as if it would flip over. Not only did we have the instability of the trailer, but we were also traveling through mountains. There were no side rails or shoulders along the road. Peering out the window, I could see straight down the mountain to what looked like a bottomless canyon. By the end of two days, fear had almost paralyzed me.

Fear of heights was not new to me. I remember, as a child, trying to climb the steps of a forest tower. I was only able to climb to about the third step before I carefully backed myself down. The higher I had climbed, the more the fear took over.

Now, many years later, as an adult, I was still fighting the same battle. Around 2:00 A.M. we stopped at a motel for the night. Someone said to me, "Barbara, if you think this is bad, wait until tomorrow. The worst is ahead." That was all I needed to hear! This was not a word that comforted me, exhorted or edified me (see 1 Cor. 14:3). How could I handle the next day's drive if it was worse than what I had already been through? My knuckles were white from holding on so tightly.

I went to bed but did not sleep. All night I tossed and turned, dreading the next day. In the morning, as we drove out from the motel to begin our day's journey, I picked up my Bible. Turning to Psalm 91, I began to read:

> He who dwells in the shelter of the Most High will abide in the shadow of the Almighty. I will say to the LORD, "My refuge and my fortress, My God, in whom I trust!" For it is He who delivers you from the snare of the trapper, and from the deadly pestilence. He will cover you with His pinions, and under His wings you may seek refuge; His faithfulness is a shield and bulwark. You will not be afraid of the terror by night, or of the arrow that flies by day (Ps. 91:1-5).

I carefully laid the Bible on the car seat next to me and closed my eyes. Tears streamed down my face, and I could no longer see to read. As I put my head back against the seat, I began to pray. "Lord, I have done everything I know to do. I have quoted your Word. I have bound everything I know to bind. I have loosed everything I know to loose (see Matt. 16:19). Nothing has worked for me. If you don't set me free from this fear, I don't know what I will do. I feel as if I can't keep going, and yet I cannot turn back. Please, release me from this torment."

About 15 minutes later, I felt something break off and lift from me. This startled me. Never had I experienced anything like it! I sat up in my seat and opened my eyes to see what had happened. I looked out the side window of the car and saw huge mountains in the distance. Waterfalls poured down the side of the mountains into a deep valley below us. Majestic trees covered the mountains. "How beautiful!" I cried out. "Look at these mountains! God made them so beautiful for us to enjoy." What had happened to me? The same thing that had caused me fear and torment 15 minutes earlier had suddenly become a thing of beauty.

The Lord had delivered me from a fear of heights that had followed me all my life. For the first time, I could experience the sheer joy of being in high places. Today I minister in many places, such as Malaysia, where we often hold meetings at the top of high mountains. The highest spot at the top of the Swiss Alps is one of my favorite places. I love glassed-in elevators. It is common for me to find myself on the highest floors of hotels and skyscrapers. Unless the Lord had delivered me from a spirit of fear, I would not be able to fulfill the destiny He has for me. Multitudes of others cannot fulfill their destiny because of fear.

The ministry of deliverance is essential to the Church. It is part of our birthright as believers.

A COMPLETE SALVATION

When Jesus purchased salvation through His death, burial and resurrection, He also purchased deliverance. *Vine's Dictionary* defines "salvation" as "deliverance, preservation; material or temporal deliverance from danger and apprehension; safety, health; spiritual and eternal deliverance granted immediately by God to those who accept His conditions of repentance and faith in the Lord Jesus Christ, in whom alone it is to be obtained and upon confession of Him as Lord."[1]

Deliverance is part of our salvation experience. Jesus made a way for believers to be whole in body, soul and spirit:

> Now may the God of peace Himself sanctify you entirely; and may your spirit and soul and body be preserved complete, without blame at the coming of our Lord Jesus Christ (1 Thess. 5:23).

Jesus not only purchased eternal life for us at Calvary; He also purchased freedom from demonic bondage and healing for our minds and bodies. He made a way for believers to be completely whole.

Jesus Christ made a way for all believers to be whole in body, soul and spirit.

Often we hear 2 Corinthians 5:17 quoted to new believers: "Therefore if any man is in Christ, he is a new creature; the old things passed away; behold, new things have come." These babes in Christ are excited to hear such good news. Never again will they be the same! Never again will they think old thoughts or say old words! Sometimes this is true for a period of time; then one day they wake up with old thoughts running through their heads. Soon after, they find themselves reacting to situations in an old way. Old, ugly words pour out of their mouths. They become confused, wondering what happened. Weren't old things supposed to have passed away and all things become new?

These people were not told that salvation is a process. Eternal life is an instantaneous experience, but we grow into the fullness of salvation. The human spirit, previously dead, came alive at the time of salvation. God put His life in our spirit, and nothing else can live there. But the body and soul are different. They must now yield to the life of God living in our spirit before they are completely whole. The soul—containing the mind, will and emotions—needs to be healed and renewed by the Word of God, while the body must be continually offered to God as a holy sacrifice (see Rom. 12:1,2).

I like the way Doris Wagner explains the threefold makeup of man:

> The spirit is the portion of a person that lives forever—it's the life that God breathed into Adam as described in Genesis 2:7. It has also been described by many as the residence of the Holy Spirit when regeneration takes place.
>
> The soul of a person is more complex. It houses such things as the emotions, mind, will, five senses and personality. It is from the soul that the real person, personality and behavior come forth. I believe that Satan can bring bondage to the body at times. Jesus mentions a "spirit of infirmity" in Luke 13:11,12 that caused a woman to be bent over for 18 years.
>
> More common, however, are bondages that afflict the soul, usually involving an emotion such as hatred or a behavior such as an addiction. David says in Psalm 41:4, "Heal my soul for I have sinned against you." This seems to imply that some bad choice was made that brought a problem to David's soul and it seemed to have lingered until David asked for its removal.[2]

Sometimes there is a battle for the body and soul to be completely healed and set free. For years I have heard people say that Christians cannot have a demon. It is true that no demon can live in our spirit; God's Spirit lives in our spirits, and He will not share that place with anything unclean. But demonic bondage can exist in our souls or bodies. Getting rid of these demonic spirits is the purpose for the ministry of deliverance.

The Church is beginning to wake up and realize the need for, and the availability of, deliverance. For too long we have ignored or refused to believe in the presence of demonic spirits. I remember many years ago listening to a missionary tell stories about the country where he was ministering. Included in his testimony were stories of people in that country who were demonized. He ended his time of sharing by making this statement: "The people in the United States are too cultured to have demonic spirits."

How can we miss it? American minds are being tormented, addictions are on the rise, crime and violent behavior are out of control, ministers are in bondage to pornography, and divorce in the Church is on par with the world. We must recognize what we are dealing with! Christians *are* in bondage.

But the good news is that they can be set free!

When we look at the life of Jesus, we see Him casting out demons. In fact, much of His earthly ministry involved setting people free from demons:

> The news about Him went out into all Syria; and they brought to Him all who were ill, taken with various diseases and pains, demoniacs, epileptics, paralytics; and He healed them (Matt. 4:24).

> When evening had come, they brought to Him many who were demon-possessed; and He cast out the spirits with a word, and healed all who were ill (Matt. 8:16).

The demons began to entreat Him, saying, "If You are going to cast us out, send us into the herd of swine." And He said to them, "Begone!" And they came out, and went into the swine, and behold, the whole herd rushed down the steep bank into the sea and perished in the waters (Matt. 8:31-32).

Jesus came as our model. Whatever He did, He instructed those who would follow Him to do the same. He ministered deliverance to the captives, and He instructed His followers to free demonized people. We have been commanded by Jesus to minister deliverance to those who need to be set free:

Heal the sick, raise the dead, cleanse the lepers, cast out demons; freely you received, freely give (Matt. 10:8).

These signs will accompany those who have believed: in My name they will cast out demons, they will speak with new tongues (Mark 16:17).

And He called the twelve together, and gave them power and authority over all the demons and to heal diseases (Luke 9:1).

FORGIVENESS IS A KEY

Forgiveness is a major key to deliverance. Failure to forgive can result in mental torment:

And his lord was wroth, and delivered him to the tormentors, till he should pay all that was due unto him. So likewise shall my heavenly Father do also unto you, if ye from your hearts forgive not every one his brother their trespasses (Matt. 18:34,35, *KJV*).

Forgiveness may need to begin as an act of the will. When we're hurting, we don't always feel like forgiving. In those times we can ask the Lord to grace us with the ability to forgive. His grace releases the power to allow our will (part of the soul) to forgive, even when the feelings of forgiveness are absent. Since Jesus commanded us to forgive, we must forgive out of obedience.

According to Jesus, we also must forgive in order to be forgiven by the Lord. A person who is unwilling to forgive cannot expect to be forgiven by God:

> Whenever you stand praying, forgive, if you have anything against anyone; so that your Father also who is in heaven may forgive you your transgressions. ["But if you do not forgive, neither will your Father who is in heaven forgive your transgressions"] (Mark 11:25,26).

Sometimes we ask, "Just how many times must I forgive this person?" Jesus gave us the answer:

> Then Peter came and said to Him, "Lord, how often shall my brother sin against me and I forgive him? Up to seven times?" Jesus said to him, "I do not say to you, up to seven times, but up to seventy times seven" (Matt.18:21,22).

Jesus was not saying we must forgive 490 times—that after 490 times, we no longer need to forgive. The number seven in the Bible stands for completion. We forgive until our forgiveness is complete. Sometimes that requires staying on our knees and forgiving over and over until we have forgiven a wrong from the depths of our heart. The more deeply we forgive, the more healing, joy, peace and love we will experience in our lives.

Forgiveness does not mean that we proclaim what the other person did was right. God never requires us to call evil "good." I encourage people who are hurting to separate the person from the evil deed. Hate the deed but forgive the person. When we are willing to release forgiveness, we are ready to be set free. There are times when a spirit of unforgiveness or hate may need to be bound before we can forgive (see Matt. 16:19). A demonic spirit may be hindering our will. After binding the spirit, we are able to choose to forgive. Feelings of forgiveness may not be present, but we have the ability to choose to forgive.

When praying for someone who needs deliverance, we must first lead the person in a confession of Jesus as Lord over every area of his or her life. Then we can lead the person in a prayer of forgiveness:

> *I confess that I have unforgiveness toward (name the people).*
> *I have been hurt, and I now hold resentment, bitterness and*
> *anger in my heart. I recognize this is sin. Therefore, I repent for*
> *my sin of unforgiveness, and I choose to forgive all these people*
> *who have hurt me. I pray this in Jesus' name. Amen.*

Do you hold unforgiveness toward yourself? Perhaps you feel responsible for something you could not prevent. It is important that you forgive yourself. Here is a sample prayer:

> *Lord, I choose to forgive myself for the things I have done. I ask*
> *You to forgive me for the wrongs I have done and forgive me for*
> *my attitudes toward others. Forgive me for hating myself. I am*
> *Your creation, and I will not hate what You have made. Thank*
> *You for loving me and making me Your child. I pray this in*
> *Jesus' name. Amen.*

Although God has never done anything wrong, we can hold resentment toward God. We may have expected God to do something He did not do. In that case, Satan was the source of evil, not God. It is important that we be honest and release forgiveness toward God when we harbor such feelings. We can pray like this:

> *Father, I recognize that You are a good and loving God. You are not responsible for my problems. You are the answer to my problems. Satan is the source of evil. Please forgive me for blaming You. I ask You to set me free. I pray this in Jesus' name. Amen.*

When doing the ministry of deliverance, working with a team is preferable. Two or three people can form a very effective team. While two are discerning and praying for the person, the third can be interceding. I strongly suggest—and make it a personal practice—never to minister deliverance alone. If necessary, you can bind spirits and schedule a later time for deliverance.

Jesus gave believers the authority to bind and loose:

> I will give you the keys of the kingdom of heaven; and whatever you shall bind on earth shall be bound in heaven, and whatever you shall loose on earth shall be loosed in heaven (Matt. 16:19).

The Greek word for "bind" is *deo*, meaning "to tie; bind; imprison; put in chains."[3] Jesus gave believers the authority to bind, imprison and put in chains the power of the enemy.

He also gave believers the authority to loose captives. "Loose" is from the Greek word *luo*, meaning "to release; to dissolve; destroy; unbind; untie."[4] When people receive deliverance, the power of the enemy is destroyed and dissolved. Captives are unbound and released from demonic powers.

Binding and loosing means praying for deliverance. We begin setting a captive free by binding all powers of darkness that have bound the one we are praying for. We then loose all powers of heaven at our disposal and ask the Lord to release the power of the Holy Spirit to empower us to deliver. Always use the name of Jesus when praying. His name is our key to authority.

It is also important to ask the Father to assign angels to assist during the time of deliverance (see Heb. 1:14). Often, while ministering deliverance, I have witnessed the manifest power of angels. At times people receiving ministry have tried to run from the room, but they were held in place by an invisible force: ministering angels. Other times they tried to pick up objects to throw at me but were unable to do so. Although I did not see the angels, I saw the results of their presence. The angels rendered the demonic spirits powerless so they could not become violent during the time of ministry.

Jesus did not give us a formula for deliverance in His Word. However, He did give us principles to follow. Peter Horrobin writes:

> There is no doubt that Jesus saw deliverance as a vital part of his ministry and strategic to his mission as the Messiah. Deliverance ministry demonstrated to the world his absolute authority over Satan and the powers of darkness. This simple fact is at the root of all the opposition there is to the practice of deliverance ministry in the Church.
>
> Then, in Luke 9:1,2, it is recorded that he shared this authority with his disciples. They were the first to be given his power and authority both to heal the sick and to cast out demons. But just as the Gospel accounts give no detailed instructions as to how Jesus expected the disciples to heal people from sicknesses and diseases,

neither do they give any instructions on how to deliver people from demons![5]

Jesus commanded us, as believers, to cast out demons. Although He did not give us a formula for deliverance ministry, He did give us the authority to fulfill our mission:

> And He called the twelve together, and gave them power and authority over all the demons and to heal diseases. And He sent them out to proclaim the kingdom of God and to perform healing (Luke 9:1,2).

I remember a young man who came to me for deliverance several years ago. Robert had been involved in Satanism but had recently received Jesus as his Lord and Savior. In the intervening weeks he had been experiencing demonic harassment. I asked him to briefly share with me about his life, his involvement in the occult and the current problems he was having. After he prayed prayers of forgiveness, we read a few Scripture passages proclaiming that Jesus had the authority to set him free. As we were reading, I noticed a look of terror on Robert's face.

"Robert, you're afraid," I said.

"Yes," he replied. "I am."

"May I tell you why you're afraid?" I asked. When he nodded, I went on. "You're afraid because you've seen the power of Satan, but you've never seen the power of God."

"You're right," Robert replied. "I've never seen the power of God."

"You're about to see it," I said.

For the next couple of hours, the power of the Lord was present to set Robert free. At times he would try to get up and run, due to the demonic hold on his life. Yet his feet were unable to move. The power of angels was holding him, while Jesus set him free.

Tremendous joy filled Robert at the end of the ministry time. His face looked different. Rage, anger and hate no longer controlled him. He was free to be the young man God created him to be—a child of God.

BREAKING THE YOKE OF BONDAGE

The anointing by the power of the Holy Spirit will break the yoke of Satan and liberate people (see Luke 4:18,19). A picture of deliverance can be seen in what I call a "fat-bull anointing." Most people do not like the word "fat." They prefer words like "skinny," "slim" and "narrow." However, this is one time you will love the word "fat"!

The word "fatness" often refers to grease, liquid or oil. But, metaphorically, it refers to a fat bull that has cast off its yoke and broken loose.[6] That is a picture of the anointing for deliverance:

> So it will be in that day, that his burden will be removed from your shoulders and his yoke from your neck, and the yoke will be broken because of fatness (Isa. 10:27).

The *King James Version* translates the word "fatness" as "anointing":

> And it shall come to pass in that day, that his burden shall be taken away from off thy shoulder, and his yoke from off thy neck, and the yoke shall be destroyed because of the anointing.

God's people are going to become slippery and greasy in the anointing for deliverance! They will get so fat in the anointing of God that they will break out of every yoke that has bound them.

God will anoint them so powerfully that they can help break the yokes off others.

Don't you just love the word "fat" now? May the Lord empower us with a fat-bull anointing to set the captives free!

DISCUSSION QUESTIONS

1. Have you ever experienced a tormenting fear? What were some of the symptoms? What did you do? Do you still have the same fear?
2. Discuss the difference between salvation and eternal life.
3. Give a biblical example of a demonic bondage that affects the body.
4. How can a person forgive when they do not feel like forgiving? How many times should a person forgive?
5. What is binding and loosing?
6. Are you willing to do as Jesus did and set the captives free?

Chapter Twelve

Faith for the Anointing

Our Christian organization desperately needed a larger space. The number of people attending the monthly meetings was continuing to increase. We were now packed to capacity in our meeting room. We had no choice but to move into a new location.

KNOWING GOD'S WILL

I yearned to know the exact place the Lord had for us. Our board members spent several weeks praying and fasting to discern the Lord's direction. After much prayer, we felt we had the Lord's leading to lease a space in a hotel. Our advisory board was in full agreement with our decision. As the leader, however, I wanted to be absolutely sure.

What will happen if we move to the wrong location? I wondered. *Would people still come to the meetings if we were in the wrong place? Was it possible we were simply moving to a convenient place, that we had not really heard the Lord?*

Questions flooded my mind as I drove to meet with the sales manager of the hotel. Crying out to God, I continued to pray for His wisdom and direction. "Lord, help me to know Your will. More than anything else in life, I want to be in Your will. Somehow, confirm that this decision is Your perfect will for us."

Pulling into the parking lot of the hotel, I noticed a marquee for the church across the street. On it were these words: "Why are ye fearful, O ye of little faith?" (Matt. 8:26, *KJV*). I sat there for a long time looking at the sign. The scripture on the sign wasn't for just anyone. It had been put there for me!

This verse may have seemed like a rebuke to many who read it while driving past the church. For me, it provided comfort. It was true that my faith needed to increase. It was true that I had doubted the Lord's direction. Even His rebuke became a thing of love, as He pressed me into a greater level of faith. I sat in the car for some time, thanking Him for confirming His direction to me. Little did I know that I would need an even greater level of faith in the days ahead!

OPERATING IN FAITH

We will never be able to walk in the fullness of the anointing and fulfill our assignment from the Lord without faith operating in our lives. Jesus walked with His disciples and taught them for three and a half years, but they did not always understand what He was saying to them.

After Jesus rose from the dead, He appeared to them as they were eating. Then, just before He commissioned them, He rebuked them for their lack of faith:

> He reproached them for their unbelief and hardness of heart, because they had not believed those who had seen Him after He had risen (Mark 16:14).

Then Jesus commissioned His disciples with what in the natural seemed an impossible task:

> Go therefore and make disciples of all the nations, baptizing them in the name of the Father and the Son and the Holy Spirit, teaching them to observe all that I commanded you (Matt. 28:19,20).

Jesus knew they would never be able to fulfill their assignment without faith, so He assured them, "I am with you always, even to the end of the age" (Matt. 28:20).

It is no different today. We will never be able to walk in the supernatural anointing that Jesus taught and demonstrated without faith operating in our lives. Hebrews gives a good definition for faith: "Now faith is the assurance of things hoped for, the conviction of things not seen" (Heb. 11:1). According to this definition, faith is in the present tense. We don't have to go out and get it. It *is*. We have only to contact the source of faith, Jesus.

Here are some other definitions for faith:

> Being persuaded, belief. . . . Miraculous faith or that faith in Christ to which, when the gospel was first propagated, was annexed the gift of working miracles.[1]

It is easy to see from these definitions that there is no human strength involved in the operation of faith. Faith is simply the functioning of God in and through us. In the release of faith, God does something supernatural on our behalf.

One type of faith is found in both Christian and non-Christian people. We sometimes call this *general faith*. I spend a lot of time flying on planes with other people, a large percentage of them unbelievers (at least, so far as believing in God is concerned). When these unbelievers board the plane, they have faith that the plane will fly. They believe it will get them safely to their destination, or they would not get on the plane.

Unbelievers work every day, believing that a paycheck will be given to them. Otherwise, they would not bother going to work. They are operating in general faith.

Believers also operate in general faith. They fly the same planes as unbelievers. They are faithful to work all week, and they expect a paycheck. Believers operate in general faith when they pray and expect answers to their prayers:

> And without faith it is impossible to please Him, for he who comes to God must believe that He is, and that He is a rewarder of those who seek Him (Heb. 11:6).

As I think back to when I received salvation, I have full knowledge of experiencing faith. The church I attended taught that I could not save myself. They told me that only faith in what Jesus had done could save me. I should have died for my sin; yet He paid the price by dying on a cross and conquering death, hell and the grave. Jesus did not stay dead but rose victoriously from the grave, and He is now seated at the right hand of the Father in heaven. He did this so that I could live forever with Him.

The faith that I experienced in receiving salvation through the finished work of Jesus is a second type of faith, known as *saving faith*:

> For by grace you have been saved through faith; and that not of yourselves, it is the gift of God; not as a result of works, that no one should boast (Eph. 2:8,9).

I cannot take credit for the faith I had to be saved. Saving faith is a gift of God, and it was given to me so that I could receive salvation. Salvation is totally from the Lord. It is all Him, and none of it is of me. None of my good works could save me. How wonderful is the grace and mercy of the Lord!

A third type of faith is the *faith that produces the fruit of the Spirit* in us:

> But the fruit of the Spirit is love, joy, peace, patience, kindness, goodness, faithfulness, gentleness, self-control; against such things there is no law (Gal. 5:22,23).

Fruit of the Spirit has an ability to grow in a Christian's life. However, its growth is not automatic. As we walk in a consistent life with Jesus, enjoying fellowship with the Holy Spirit and feeding daily from the Scriptures, the fruit of the Spirit will increase. Christians need these ingredients to mature the fruit. Faith, as fruit of the Spirit, will then increase:

> I am the vine, you are the branches; he who abides in Me, and I in him, he bears much fruit, for apart from Me you can do nothing (John 15:5).

A fourth kind of faith is the *gift of faith*: "To another faith by the same Spirit, and to another gifts of healing by the one Spirit" (1 Cor. 12:9). The same verse in *The Amplified Bible* reads "[wonder-working] faith." I love this gift! The gift of faith is involved in the receiving and releasing of miracles. But the gift of faith is different from the working of miracles. Kenneth Hagin explains the difference:

> The gift of faith is a supernatural endowment by the Spirit whereby that which is uttered or desired by man or spoken by God shall eventually come to pass. . . . The gift of faith is distinct from the working of miracles, though both gifts produce miracles. One of them is

active, and the other is passive. Working of miracles is active; the gift of faith doesn't work but passively receives. In other words, the difference between working of miracles and the gift of faith is that one *does*, and the other *receives*.[2]

When the gift of faith is in operation, nothing may be seen for the moment. However, faith will abide for a long time, and eventually the result of faith will manifest.

The operation of the gift of faith can be used to provide personal protection, just as Daniel received protection in the lion's den as a result of his faith:

Then Daniel spoke to the king, "O king, live forever! My God sent His angel and shut the lions' mouths and they have not harmed me, inasmuch as I was found innocent before Him; and also toward you, O king, I have committed no crime." Then the king was very pleased and gave orders for Daniel to be taken up out of the den. So Daniel was taken up out of the den, and no injury whatever was found on him, because he had trusted in his God (Dan. 6:21-23).

Others were then thrown in the lion's den and died. Even though Daniel's circumstances seemed hopeless, he was preserved because of his faith.

Jesus and the disciples were preserved from the storm at sea through the gift of faith:

He rebuked the wind and said to the sea, "Hush, be still." And the wind died down and it became perfectly calm. And He said to them, "Why are you so timid? How is it that you have no faith?" (Mark 4:39,40).

Jesus had faith that the winds and sea would obey Him. He has given believers the same authority and faith for their protection.

SHIFTING TO A NEW LEVEL

Living in east Texas for a number of years taught me much about tornadoes. Many times tornadoes passed right over our house. When that happened, I would gather the children in the center of the house where there were no windows. As we listened to the radio reports, I prayed and took authority over the funnel clouds and commanded them to dissipate and not touch down.

One night I was driving about 100 miles to teach a spiritual warfare seminar at a prison. As I drove into Jacksonville, Texas, I found that trees were lying on the ground, roofs were off buildings and all electricity was off in the town. As I continued driving toward the prison, I turned on my car radio for updates on the weather. At one point it was announced that a tornado had been spotted over the exact place where I was driving. The announcer warned listeners to take cover immediately, but I was on an open stretch of road with no place to hide. So I prayed, "I command this tornado to stay in the sky. I forbid you to touch down in Jesus' name." I continued driving to the prison, feeling a sense of peace, despite the danger I was in. The gift of faith was in operation, and I knew I was protected.

Sometimes I describe the gift of faith as being like a car shifting gears. There is a sense of shifting into a new level of faith, and you know you have the miracle. You do not have to work to believe; you simply know you will receive what you have asked for.

The gift of faith can also be used for raising the dead. Three things need to happen in order to raise someone from the dead:

1. The person's spirit must return to the body.
2. The person's body must be reanimated.

3. Substantial healing must occur to overcome the effects of whatever accident or illness killed the person.

These three things correspond to the New Testament gifts of faith, miracles and healing, although faith is required in the use of all spiritual gifts. During his lifetime, Smith Wigglesworth was used mightily by God to raise several people from the dead.

The gift of faith is exercised when casting out demons. The discerning of spirits will reveal which spirit is present, but the gift of faith will force the demon to leave.

The gift of faith is also activated when we prophesy. We prophesy according to our faith, and many times we prophesy out of the gift of faith. Miracles are then released.

God gives the gift of faith in certain times and circumstances, according to His will. If we will apply the faith we have, we will find ourselves shifting into the gift of faith in those times when it is needed.

DEVELOPING OUR FAITH

If faith is so important, how do we develop it? In the same way we must feed a baby so he or she will grow, we must also feed and water our faith for it to grow.

> For through the grace given to me I say to everyone among you not to think more highly of himself than he ought to think; but to think so as to have sound judgment, as God has allotted to each a measure of faith (Rom. 12:3).

Each believer has already been given a measure of faith. That means every believer has been given an *adequate* portion of faith. The important thing is to develop the faith we already have.

When our children were small, they were always concerned about receiving their adequate portion of dessert. Whenever cake or pie was served, each child would measure his or her piece against the others. Sometimes we are that way in our spiritual lives. We are always looking to see if our faith is as great as that of other believers. God has given each of us an adequate portion of faith. We do not need to get *more* faith. We need only to use and develop the faith we have.

Faith grows as the Word of God is put into our heart (see Col. 1:9). It is difficult for me to have faith if I am not sure the thing I am believing for is God's will. Studying God's Word helps me to know His will for my life. When I know His will, I can have faith to see it happen.

Faith develops when it is put into action. Sometimes we must *do* something with what we believe: "For just as the body without the spirit is dead, so also faith without works is dead" (Jas. 2:26). When our oldest son, Brian, started learning to walk alone, for several months he walked by holding onto anything close by. When there was nothing to hold onto, he would crawl. One day we decided we needed to encourage him to walk without any support.

As Dale and I sat on the floor, we held our arms out to Brian and called, "Come here, baby. You can do it. You can walk." At first, Brian merely looked at us. He then looked at the sofa he was holding. For several minutes we watched, as he first looked at the comfortable support of the sofa and then at us a short distance away—with no handholds between him and us. Finally, faith rose up in him. His little hands let go of the sofa, and he stepped away to walk. After only a few steps, he started to fall. We quickly grabbed him and cheered, "You made it. You walked!" A big grin came across his face. He had put his faith into action.

Within three days, Brian was not just walking; he was running. His faith had grown, because he knew he had a father and mother who would catch him if he started to fall. We can act on what we believe, because we know our heavenly Father is there to catch us if we start to fall. He delights to see His children take action with their faith.

> # We can act on what we believe, because we know our heavenly Father is there to catch us if we start to fall.

Our faith is to work by love (see Gal. 5:6). I often find that because of fear, Christians are not ministering under the anointing of the Holy Spirit. Many are afraid of "missing God." Some are afraid that what they do will not produce the needed results. Others are afraid of what people will say.

Shortly after I came into the fullness of the Spirit, I attended a conference where a lady was speaking on the fear of God. She made a statement that forever changed my life: "You will never walk in the fear of the Lord until you lose the fear of man." That statement was like an arrow that went straight to my heart. For the first time in my life I realized that I had the fear of man in me.

I had often wondered why I was so shy and timid. I just thought some people, including myself, were born that way, while others were extroverted and outgoing. Now I had to face the facts: I was timid and shy not because that was the way God made me, but because I had the fear of man in my life. What a revelation!

For hours I lay on the floor and cried out, "I confess that I have not always been obedient to you, Lord! I have been afraid of failure.

I have feared making a mistake. I felt inadequate." My list went on and on. After this time of confession, I asked the Lord to forgive me: "Forgive me for thinking of my own reputation rather than the needs of others. Forgive me for wanting to do things to please people rather than desiring to please You." I finished by asking the Lord to help me break this habit in my life: "Remind me, Lord, when I start to operate in the fear of man. I forget so easily." It was a desperate prayer from the depths of my heart.

Later, when I was asked to stand and speak before a group of people, the Lord reminded me of that prayer. I remember how my throat tightened with fear before standing up to speak. Each time this happened the Lord would ask me, *Is this the fear of the Lord or the fear of man?* I knew then I had to make a choice. Would I allow my life to be controlled by the fear of man, or would I choose to walk in the fear of the Lord?

The symptoms of the fear of man did not go away overnight. However, I chose every time to fear the Lord rather than man. I can remember saying to God in those times, "If I fall flat on my face trying to please You, I am willing." Each time, He sustained me in my acts of obedience. The more I chose to walk in the fear of the Lord, the weaker the fear of man became in my life. Today people are amazed when they hear my story. It is difficult for them to believe that I came from such a timid, fearful background.

As I let Him fill me more and more with His love, fear was forced to flee. God's love completely removed fear from my life.

There is no fear in love; but perfect love casts out fear, because fear involves punishment, and the one who fears is not perfected in love (1 John 4:18).

In the same way we cheered Brian on when he was learning to walk, God the Father wants to cheer us on as we sally forth in our adventures of faith.

The anointing is fueled through faith. Just as gasoline is the fuel that causes an automobile to move forward, faith is the fuel that propels God's people forward to move in the anointing on their lives.

DISCUSSION QUESTIONS

1. Give your own definition for faith. Name the four types of faith.
2. Describe general faith and give an example from your own life.
3. Define saving faith. Tell about your experience in receiving saving faith.
4. Tell about a time when you experienced the gift of faith.
5. What are some other situations in which the gift of faith can be used?
6. What are some ways you can develop the gift of faith?
7. Have you experienced the fear of man? How have you dealt with it?

Chapter Thirteen

Transferable Anointing

A friend of mine named Peter received a substantial inheritance from his late father. After the proper paperwork had been filed, the funds were transferred to Peter's bank account. Money that had previously been owned by his father became Peter's.

Peter's father had been a rancher who spent many hard years working to buy land and equipment. His was a meager beginning, but Peter's father knew how to plant the right crops at the right time. He was able to repair machinery and keep his equipment running longer than most ranchers. Through the years, he managed to put a little money aside in order to leave a nice inheritance for his son.

Now the money had been transferred to Peter. He was at liberty to take his newly acquired assets and invest them where they would increase and multiply. By wisely using what he received, in a relatively short period of time Peter acquired more than the sum of his father's lifelong endeavors. But Peter's substantial portfolio had begun with a small transference.

PASSING ON THE GIFT

Jesus admonished his followers to take what they had received and invest it wisely (see Matt. 25:14-30). By doing so, they would receive an increase. We are able to do the same thing with the anointing.

As we exercise the anointing that is given to us, it will increase. Just as Peter received a transfer of funds from his earthly father and increased his inheritance by wisely investing those funds, so can we. We not only are able to receive an anointing from our heavenly Father, but it can also be transferred to us from others. As we exercise the use of the anointing, it continually grows into all the Lord has purposed for us.

The Bible clearly teaches that the anointing can be given to another person. Paul reminded his spiritual son Timothy not to neglect the spiritual gift he had received from Paul: "For this reason I remind you to kindle afresh the gift of God which is in you through the laying on of my hands" (2 Tim. 1:6). Paul also wrote to the Christians in Rome and expressed a desire to come to them so that he could impart a spiritual gift to them: "I long to see you in order that I may impart some spiritual gift to you, that you may be established" (Rom. 1:11). Some of the anointing on Paul was transferred to Timothy and to other believers.

The same principle of transferring the anointing can be seen elsewhere in the Bible. Moses transferred some of his anointing to Joshua. Joshua had been a warrior under Moses' leadership, but Joshua needed a new anointing for a new season in his life. Moses laid hands on him and transferred an anointing to Joshua to equip him for leadership:

Now Joshua the son of Nun was filled with the spirit of wisdom, for Moses had laid his hands on him; and the sons of Israel listened to him and did as the LORD had commanded Moses (Deut. 34:9).

The anointing is necessary spiritual equipment for fulfilling God's purpose in ministry. How sad it is to see those who have a heart for God and yet labor in their own strength. Usually they end up in discouragement and defeat. Without the anointing there is a limit to what they are able to accomplish. The Lord has made a way for believers to be fully equipped for the task He has given them.

The purpose of the fivefold gifts, or ascension gift ministries, is to equip believers for the work of the ministry:

> And He gave some as apostles, and some as prophets, and some as evangelists, and some as pastors and teachers, for the equipping of the saints for the work of service, to the building up of the body of Christ (Eph. 4:11,12).

These ministries are not called by the Lord to do the work of the ministry; rather, they are called to equip other believers to do the work of the ministry. Part of the equipping process includes transferring the anointing that will allow others to be successful in ministry. I wonder how many discouraged and defeated ministers would have a different story to tell if they had been equipped through the transference of anointing for the task the Lord had for them.

THE LAYING ON OF HANDS

One of the ways an anointing can be transferred is through the laying on of hands. This doctrine should be part of the foundation in the life of every believer (see Heb. 6:1,2). The Lord has made a way for believers to lay hands on people and release God's power to heal and set them free. This anointing is not just for those in church ministry. It is for every believer: "These signs will accompany *those who have believed*" (Mark 16:17, emphasis added).

Throughout the Old and New Testaments, we see the practice of the laying on of hands. This was done for a variety of reasons, one of which was healing. My mother-in-law, Edith, attended a Kathryn Kuhlman meeting many years ago. She was living in Pittsburgh during the time of Kuhlman's famous healing conventions. Edith's pastor had told his congregation that the people in those meetings were not really healed—they just thought they were. Edith decided to find out for herself.

Although Edith had a long-standing back problem that occasionally made it almost impossible to get out of bed, she did not attend the meeting for the purpose of being healed. She simply went to see if others were truly being healed. As Kuhlman began to speak about healings that were taking place in the audience, she pointed her finger toward the balcony where Edith was sitting and announced, "Someone is being healed from a back problem." Not expecting to be healed, Edith continued to sit in her chair. A few minutes later one of the ushers tapped her on the shoulder and asked, "Do you have a problem with your back?" After admitting her condition, Edith was escorted down the stairs and up to the platform.

Kuhlman laid hands on Edith, and the power of God ran through her body. Minutes later, she had not only been healed from a very painful back problem, but she had also been healed of varicose veins that had looked like ropes in her legs. Now she knew that it really didn't matter what the critics said. She had experienced a supernatural healing. God's healing power is available when believers lay hands on the sick—and they really do recover!

Another purpose for the laying on of hands is so that people may be filled with the Holy Spirit:

> So Ananias departed and entered the house, and after laying his hands on him said, "Brother Saul, the Lord Jesus, who appeared to you on the road by which you were coming, has sent me so that you may regain your sight, and be filled with the Holy Spirit" (Acts 9:17).

The power of the Holy Spirit is vital for accomplishing the Lord's will in our lives. Before I was filled with the Holy Spirit I had no hunger for the Word of God, and I was extremely timid. Although I was a faithful church member, I was a powerless church member.

After being filled with the Holy Spirit, my entire life changed. It seemed the sky was bluer and the birds sang more beautifully. I had an unquenchable thirst and hunger for the Lord and His Word. God's power immediately began to change me into the person He created me to be. I was not the person I thought I was. If the early Christians needed the Holy Spirit in their day, how much more do we need the power of the Holy Spirit in this day and age?

Sometimes the laying on of hands is used to impart spiritual blessings. Jesus laid His hands on children and released a blessing to them (see Matt. 19:15).

The laying on of hands is also practiced to impart spiritual gifts in a commissioning ceremony for ministry. Although Saul (later Paul) and Barnabas were already ministers at the church in Antioch, they were commissioned for a new assignment from the Lord. The leaders at Antioch laid hands on them before they sent them out to fulfill their assignment (see Acts 13:2,3). New spiritual equipment is required for a new assignment. The Bible tells us these men experienced great victories after this event.

Would we read a different story had they not had hands laid on them and received gifts necessary for the task set before them?

David Blomgren, in his book *The Laying on of Hands and Prophecy of the Presbytery*, reports scientific evidence that an impartation occurs during the laying on of hands. The first evidence came from a biochemist and enzymologist in the late 1960s. Dr. Justa Smith performed an experiment to study the effects of the laying on of hands. The theory behind the research was that if the energy force imparted in the laying on of hands is real, the change should be apparent at the enzymatic level. Dr. Smith set up several flasks filled with trypsin solution. Hands were laid on them for 75 minutes each day. Another flask was set up that was exposed to a high magnetic field. Yet another flask was filled but left untouched. The results of the test showed that the effects on the flasks that had received the laying on of hands were similar to the effects of being exposed to the magnetic field.[1]

In another test, performed by Dr. Delores Krieger, a professor at New York University, blood tests were done prior to the experiment. Those who had hands laid on them during the tests showed a significant change in their mean hemoglobin values. Those in the control group who did not have hands laid on them showed no significant difference between the pretest and posttest hemoglobin values. Krieger's tests indicate that something really happens during the laying on of hands—even in the physical realm. Blomgren goes on to stress the importance of the laying on of hands:

Secular science has provided an invaluable service to biblical truth by supporting and proving statistically what God's Word has purported for several millennia, that there is an actual impartation which occurs in the laying on of hands. Science, by its essential, empirical nature, could only examine a level of impartation in the laying on of hands that would deal with the physical and material part of man. Man, however, has not only a physical and bodily aspect, but he is composed of the immaterial, soul and spirit.

God Himself is essentially Spirit and not of material nature (see John 4:24). Therefore, it would follow that the essence of that which God would impart to man through the laying on of hands of His Spirit-filled servants would be more than an impartation of physical energy. Rather, it would be expected that God would impart a spiritual vitality, a touch of God's own life.[2]

RECEIVING THE ANOINTING THROUGH PROPHECY

Gifts and anointings can also be received through prophecy. Paul imparted spiritual gifts not only through the laying on of hands but also through prophecy (see Rom. 1:11; 1 Tim. 1:14). Often I have seen those who receive a prophetic word be released into supernatural ministry, even though prior to the prophetic word, they had been unable to minister in that dimension.

I was speaking at a meeting in the state of Washington a few years ago. At the end of one of the meetings, I noticed a lady standing at the back of the room near a door. It was difficult to see her clearly, but I knew the Lord wanted to minister a prophetic word to her. I called out, "The lady at the top of the stairs, what is your name? Sonia? Okay. Well, Sonia, I just see that God has a mighty call upon your life. God says He has made you a leader among women. And the Lord wants you to know that you are moving into a new season that He has for you. The Lord says don't look back at what you call failures and what you call mistakes, but look at the new season that He has for you. The new season the Lord is bringing you into is a good season, says the Lord. He says the plans I have for you are for good and not for evil. Know that the hand of the Lord is mighty upon you. The Lord is going to use you to bring a new liberty and a new joy to His people, and so the Lord is saying to walk forward."

Sonia started jumping up and down, screaming and laughing. She was the daughter of missionary parents and had grown up in Brazil. As a child, she had known the call of God on her life. However, circumstances had convinced her that God could never use her the way He had used her parents.

A few months later in another meeting, I prophesied over Sonia and her husband, Dick. The prophetic word had to do with their call to other nations, although Dick was not interested in either ministry or church at that time. Yet before the meeting was over, he found himself at the front of the room, being filled with the Holy Spirit. As a result of the prophetic word—

The anointing is not a style or formula used in the past or by someone else. The anointing needs to be fresh!

along with Dick and Sonia's obedience—they have since built churches and orphanages in Brazil. Sonia speaks at strategic conferences for church networks and helps equip leaders in that nation. God's people in Brazil are experiencing a new joy and liberty, as Sonia brings them out of old religious bondage. Religious rules and regulations are being replaced with a fresh life in the Spirit. An impartation for ministry occurred in Sonia and Dick's life as a result of the prophetic word, and they were equipped to fulfill God's purposes.

Sometimes those who have observed a person ministering have tried to duplicate what they have witnessed. Although we can and should learn from others, God has a unique anointing for each believer. The anointing is not a style or formula used in the past or by someone else. The anointing needs to be fresh. King David understood this. He rejoiced in the fresh anointing from the Lord for his life:

> But Thou hast exalted my horn like that of the wild ox;
> I have been anointed with fresh oil (Ps. 92:10).

HOW TO RELEASE THE ANOINTING

Once a person receives the anointing, how is it released in that person's life? Many people know they have an anointing; they just don't know how to get out of them what God has put inside! There are some very practical ways to begin releasing the anointing.

First of all, for releasing the anointing, there is no substitute for prayer and worship. Prayer puts us in direct contact with the Anointed One Himself—Jesus Christ. He is the source of the anointing, and the anointing is released as His life flows in and through us. As we spend time in worship and prayer, the anointing is allowed to flow through us:

> I shall pray with the spirit and I shall pray with the mind also; I shall sing with the spirit and I shall sing with the mind also (1 Cor. 14:15).

Young David would play the harp before Saul when the king was tormented with an evil spirit (see 1 Sam. 16:14-23). The anointing on David's music released an anointing to free Saul from the demonic spirit. Worship not only frees the anointing to flow through the worshiper, but it also releases the power of God to bring about needed change.

Also necessary for the release of the anointing is time spent in the Word of God. A good understanding of the Bible builds a strong foundation in the life of the believer. We are anointed for ministry, and all ministry should flow in obedience to the Word.

We must also learn to listen for the voice of the Lord. We can't just listen to what people are telling us; we must listen to what the Spirit of God is telling us. I remember a lady who came to me, asking for prayer that her broken arm might be healed. She told me she had been in an accident with an 18-wheel truck. I heard the Lord say to me, "Tell her to forgive the truck driver." When I told her what the Lord had spoken to me, she admitted her anger and unforgiveness toward the man. And so, contrary to her earthly circumstances, she prayed and released forgiveness. The healing was so instantaneous that she was able to have the cast removed by her doctor the next day. Later she wrote to tell me that a national Christian TV network was going to film her story in order to share her miraculous healing with others. The Lord is fully aware of every situation, and He knows the answer to each problem.

I have found that it is important in receiving and releasing the anointing to seek out the company of anointed people. I don't remember where I first heard this phrase, but it is vital to an understanding of the anointing: "The anointing is more caught than taught." I encourage people to hang around with anointed people, those who are fully alive with the Spirit of God. We will receive from those with whom we associate.

We must also remember to be faithful where we are. God always honors faithfulness. Some people run from church to church and from conference to conference, looking for some kind of door to open that unleashes the anointing in their lives. However, they never develop spiritual roots, and years later they are still wondering why ministry has never developed for them. We must learn to bloom where we are planted. King David was first anointed among his own brothers. We should first be anointed in our own household and among our own family. This may be our natural or spiritual family. The anointing should work at home before we try to export it.

Another helpful step I have found in releasing the anointing is to build up my faith before laying hands on anyone. I do this by praying until my level of faith rises up: "But you, beloved, building yourselves up on your most holy faith, praying in the Holy Spirit" (Jude 20). Many times I can sense the anointing of the Lord rising up; my faith becomes stronger, and I know God is ready to perform a miracle. Once my faith is at a level where I can believe the Lord to do what He wants for someone, I lay hands on that person to release the power of the anointing. I once heard someone say, "We don't need to lay empty hands on empty heads." I agree. Our hands should release an impartation of the life and power of God for whatever the need is in that person's life.

Finally, we must allow the anointing of the Lord to flow through us to others. Remember, the anointing is transferable. In our flesh we can do nothing. We can never trust in ourselves to heal, prophesy or meet people's needs. It takes the supernatural power of God to release miracles. Knowing this, we must always keep our focus on the Lord and depend on Him to do the work. We can allow Him to use our hands, our mouth and our anointing to perform the needed miracle. God does not have a Plan B. He has only a Plan A. His plan is for the Church—that's you and me—to be an extension of Him on the earth. Whatever Jesus did, we are to do. We make ourselves available, and then He empowers us with the anointing.

As I look at God's track record through the years, I see that it is perfect. I can trust Him. When I have done my part in praying, worshiping, studying the Word, listening for His voice, seeking out anointed men and women of God and building up my faith, I can always trust the Lord to do His part. And when the power of the anointing is released, He always gets the glory!

DISCUSSION QUESTIONS

1. Name two ways the anointing can be transferred from one person to another.
2. Discuss some of the things that can be received as a result of the laying on of hands.
3. Why are worship and prayer effective in releasing the anointing?
4. Discuss the importance of a strong foundation in the Word. Why is a biblical foundation necessary in releasing the anointing?
5. Why is it important to listen for God's voice when ministering to others?
6. Have you ever experienced any physical manifestations while praying for others? Describe what you experienced. What happened as a result of your ministry?
7. What should you do before laying hands on another person?
8. Whom are you trusting to get the job done?

Chapter 1

1. Kelly Varner, *Understanding Types, Shadows, and Names* (Shippensburg, PA: Destiny Image, 1996), vol. 1, p. 45.
2. Benny Hinn, *The Anointing* (Nashville, TN: Thomas Nelson, 1992), p. 159.
3. *New American Standard Hebrew-Aramaic and Greek Dictionaries*, CD-ROM, s.v. "tavek."
4. Kelly Varner, *Corporate Anointing* (Shippensburg, PA: Destiny Image, 1998), p. 2.
5. Hinn, *The Anointing*, p. 74.

Chapter 2

1. Robert Heidler, *Experiencing the Spirit* (Ventura, CA: Renew Books, 1998), pp. 60, 61.
2. John Wimber and Kevin Springer, *Power Points* (San Francisco: Harper San Francisco, 1991), p. 148.
3. Hinn, *The Anointing*, p. 11.

Chapter 3

1. Lori Wilke, *The Costly Anointing* (Shippensburg, PA: Destiny Image, 1991), p. 16.
2. Heidler, *Experiencing the Spirit*, p. 48.

Chapter 4

1. Frank Damazio, *Developing the Prophetic Ministry* (Portland, OR: Bible Temple Publishing, 1983), p. 5.
2. Bill Hamon, *Prophets and the Prophetic Movement* (Shippensburg, PA: Destiny Image, 1990), p. 20.

Chapter 5

1. *Webster's New World College Dictionary,* fourth edition, s.v. "ambassador."
2. James Strong, *Strong's Exhaustive Concordance of the Bible, Greek Dictionary of the New Testament* (McLean, VA: MacDonald Publishing Company, n.d.), p. 15.
3. Mark Hanby, *You Have Not Many Fathers* (Shippensburg, PA: Destiny Image, 1996), p. 10.
4. John and Paula Sanford, *Restoring the Christian Family* (Tulsa, OK: Victory House, 1979), p. 168.
5. Barbara Wentroble, *A People of Destiny: Finding Your Place in God's Apostolic Order* (Colorado Springs, CO: Wagner Publications, 2000), pp. 42-48.

Chapter 6

1. *Webster's New World College Dictionary,* fourth edition, s.v. "intercede."
2. James Strong, *Strong's Exhaustive Concordance of the Bible, Hebrew and Chaldee Dictionary* (McLean, VA: MacDonald Publishing Company, n.d.), p. 93.
3. Dutch Sheets, *Intercessory Prayer* (Ventura, CA: Regal Books, 1996), p. 58.
4. Barbara Wentroble, *Prophetic Intercession* (Ventura, CA: Renew Books, 1999), pp. 76, 77.
5. Elizabeth Alves, *Becoming a Prayer Warrior* (Ventura, CA: Renew Books, 1999), p. 22.
6. Frank Damazio, *Seasons of Revival* (Portland, OR: Bible Temple Publishing, 1996), p. 363.
7. Ruth Specter Lascelle, *A Dwelling Place for God* (Seattle, WA: Rock of Israel Press, 1973), pp. 235, 236.

Chapter 7

1. *Webster's New World College Dictionary,* fourth edition, s.v. "synergy."
2. Varner, *Corporate Anointing,* pp. 136, 137.

Chapter 8

1. Bill Hamon, *The Eternal Church* (Point Washington, FL: Christian International Publishers, 1990), p. 91.
2. *Webster's New World College Dictionary,* fourth edition, s.v. "clergy."
3. Ibid., s.v. "laity."
4. Rich Marshall, *God at Work* (Shippensburg, PA: Destiny Image, 2000), pp. 4, 5.
5. Frank Damazio, *Crossing Rivers, Taking Cities* (Ventura, CA: Regal Books, 1999), p. 201.
6. I discuss prophetic acts in greater detail in *Prophetic Intercession.*

Chapter 9

1. Wentroble, *A People of Destiny*, p. 50.
2. Ibid., p. 54, quoting John Wimber.

Chapter 10

1. George Barna, *The Habits of Highly Effective Churches* (Ventura, CA: Issachar Resources, 1998), pp. 119, 120.
2. Rick Renner, *Merchandising the Anointing: Developing Discernment for These Last Days* (Tulsa, OK: Rick Renner Ministries, 1990), p. 14.
3. Jon L. Pierce and John W. Newstrom, *Leaders and the Leadership Process* (Boston: Irwin McGraw-Hill, 2000), p. 25.
4. Watchman Nee, *The Latent Power of the Soul* (New York: Christian Fellowship Publishers, 1972), p. 52.

Chapter 11

1. *Vine's Expository Dictionary of New Testament Words*, s.v. "salvation."
2. Doris Wagner, *How to Cast Out Demons* (Colorado Springs, CO: Wagner Institute for Practical Ministry, 1999), p. 38.
3. *Greek Dictionary of the New American Standard Exhaustive Dictionary*, CD-ROM, s.v. "bind."
4. Ibid., s.v. "loose."
5. Peter Horrobin, *Healing Through Deliverance 2: The Practical Ministry* (Kent, England: Sovereign World, 1995), p. 31.
6. Spiros Zodhiates, "Lexical Aids to the Old Testament," *The Hebrew-Greek Key Study Bible, New American Standard Version* (Chattanooga, TN: AMG Publishers, 1990), pp. 1786, 1787.

Chapter 12

1. Spiros Zodhiates, "Lexicon to the New Testament," *The Hebrew-Greek Key Study Bible, New American Standard Version* (Chattanooga, TN: AMG Publishers, 1990), p. 1867.
2. Kenneth E. Hagin, *Concerning Spiritual Gifts* (Tulsa, OK: Faith Library Publications, 1984), p. 73.

Chapter 13

1. David K. Blomgren, *The Laying on of Hands and Prophecy of the Presbytery* (Portland, OR: Bible Temple Publications, 1979), pp. 15, 16.
2. Ibid., p. 16.

To contact Barbara Wentroble or for more information
about Wentroble Christian Ministries, please write or call:

WENTROBLE CHRISTIAN MINISTRIES

P.O. BOX 382107

DUNCANVILLE, TEXAS 75138

(972) 283-9199

FAX (972) 283-9198

E-MAIL: WCMIN1@AOL.COM